'MY NAME IS FRANCES!'

Her Story

by

ANNE BATCHELOR

Highgate of Beverley

Highgate Publications (Beverley) Limited
1998

THIS BOOK IS DEDICATED TO
ERNEST AND ANNIE HARRAP, THE GRANDPARENTS I NEVER KNEW,
TO WILL HARRAP, OUR 'D-DAY DODGER', ASLEEP IN ITALY,
AND TO MY DEAR MOTHER, FRANCES, WITH LOVE AND GRATITUDE.

British Library Cataloguing in Publication Data.
A catalogue record for this book is available from the British Library.

ISBN 0 948929 45 6

Published by

Highgate of Beverley

Highgate Publications (Beverley) Limited
24 Wylies Road, Beverley, HU17 7AP
Telephone (01482) 866826

Produced by

ba print

4 Newbegin, Lairgate, Beverley, HU17 8EG
Telephone (01482) 886017

Front Cover Pictures: Frances – then and now.
Back cover: Mother and daughter.

CONTENTS

FOREWORD

by **David Jackaman**
Regional Legacy Officer, The Children's Society

It was on a visit to Leeds during the course of my work with the Children's Society that I had the pleasure of meeting family historian Anne Batchelor. She invited me to visit her mother, Frances, who lived nearby in a small flat, surrounded by her family photographs and other souvenirs of a long and happy life.

Nothing unusual about that, you may think, but Frances did not have the sort of start in life that most people experience. She was only four when her mother died, so she and her brother were brought up in Homes run by The Children's Society, one of Britain's oldest children's charities, which was founded in 1881.

She is a living link with its founder, Edward Rudolf, for she possesses copies of letters written to him in 1920 about her desperate need for a home. From her tragic beginnings, thanks to the care and dedication of those who cared about her and for her, she was able to make a life for herself with a loving husband and daughter, and has now reached a contented old age.

Over the years thousands of children like Frances have been helped by The Children's Society. This is the wonderful story of what happened to just two of our children.

With David Jackaman of The Children's Society

INTRODUCTION

'Now, Mrs. Batchelor,' said the lady from Social Services, 'tell me, what is your first name?' Mum glanced at me, smiled and said firmly, 'My name is *Frances* – with an "e"!'

She is so insistent because, she says, she fears that if it is spelt as the masculine Francis she could one day find herself in a male hospital ward! Of course that could still happen in these days of mixed-sex wards, but that has always been the explanation she has given to anyone official requiring her Christian name. However, having spent time uncovering the story of her childhood, I now know that there is another deep-seated and almost forgotten reason for her forceful reply.

She has often told me that she was brought up in a children's home after the early death of her mother. When recounting stories of those long-ago days she suddenly revealed how she lost her Christian name for a number of years. 'One day,' she said, 'another little girl called Frances came to live in the Home. Matron told me that they couldn't have two girls called Frances. It would be too confusing. Because the new girl was only small, she could keep her name. "But," said Matron, "you can't be Frances any more. You will have to be – Joan".'

'I don't know where they got that name from,' said Mum. 'It certainly wasn't mine! For a while I was Joan Harrap, then another new girl arrived – called Joan! I was told that now I couldn't be Joan either. I had to be known as Fanny Harrap – which I *hated*!' How awful for her to lose her name not once but twice.

This, I believe, is why she answers officialdom's questions with such feeling. To the doctor, the Home Care Manager, the Vicar, the ladies at her Day Centre – to everyone who asks her she insists – 'My name is *Frances!*'

When I came to write this account of her family's story, that had to be the title. It is a declaration of who she is – a statement of identity.

I had intended that this book should be a companion volume to *A Batchelor's Delight*, in which I had described how I tracked my father's family back to the days of King Henry VIII. I planned to do the same kind of research of my mother's family – going back across the centuries. Instead, this book is firmly based in the twentieth century, but nevertheless tells of a search for my maternal family's story which was equally fascinating – full of the mysteries and revelations, dead ends and discoveries which make family research so addictive.

When the B.B.C., in 1989, were filming the story of my Batchelor research for their *Timewatch* series, my producer Antonia Benedek said to my mother, 'And when shall we be telling *your* story, Mrs. Batchelor?' Mum smiled modestly and said, 'Oh, no-one would be interested in *my* story!' Perhaps when you have read it, dear reader, you will disagree.

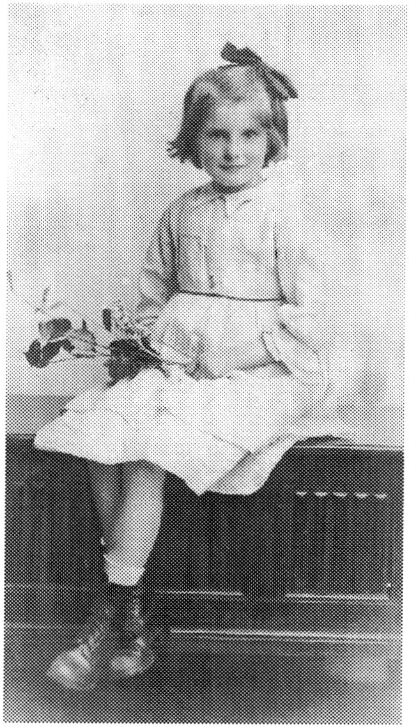

CHAPTER ONE

'A MOST IMMORAL PLACE'

Ernest Harrap was weary of funerals. Already he had buried his first two little children. Now his red-haired young wife lay in her coffin in their small back-to-back house in Duke Street, Featherstone, awaiting her burial. She was only twenty-eight and had died of double pneumonia in the worldwide outbreak of influenza of 1917. All that he had left now was his little daughter, Frances, aged four, and the baby, William, who was two. How was he going to manage to bring them up alone? Perhaps his brothers and sisters might be able to help?

His thoughts were interrupted by the sudden arrival of Frances, who came dashing in from play. Seeing the coffin – polished wood and shiny brass handles – she exclaimed in excitement, 'Ooh – have we got some new furniture?' Her innocent question must have well nigh broken his heart.

Although my mother, Frances, is now in her eighties, her memories of those far-off days are surprisingly vivid. She still has her mother's black-edged death card, for, even though her father was an impoverished miner, he had wanted to mark his young wife's passing in the correct manner. 'In Affectionate Remembrance of Annie Harrap', it reads, 'beloved wife of Ernest Harrap, who died Nov. 27, 1917 – Aged 28 yrs. Interred at Featherstone Cemetery – Dec. 1st.'

The opposite side of the card bears a simple yet painfully moving verse :

'A tender mother she has been
And many troubles she has seen.
While she lived she did her best
And now in Jesus she is blest.
Farewell, dear children, my life is past.
I lived and loved you to the last.
Since I am gone do not forsake
But love each other for my sake.'

This was followed by a pious 'Thy will be done' and the address – 4 Duke Street.

Annie Harrap with baby Frances c.1914.

Mum has only a few dim memories of her mother. 'She had lovely red hair. I remember, beside her bed, she had lots of big soda syphons. Probably she was so ill that she was past eating and that was all that she could manage. I remember ever so well being sent with our Will to fetch

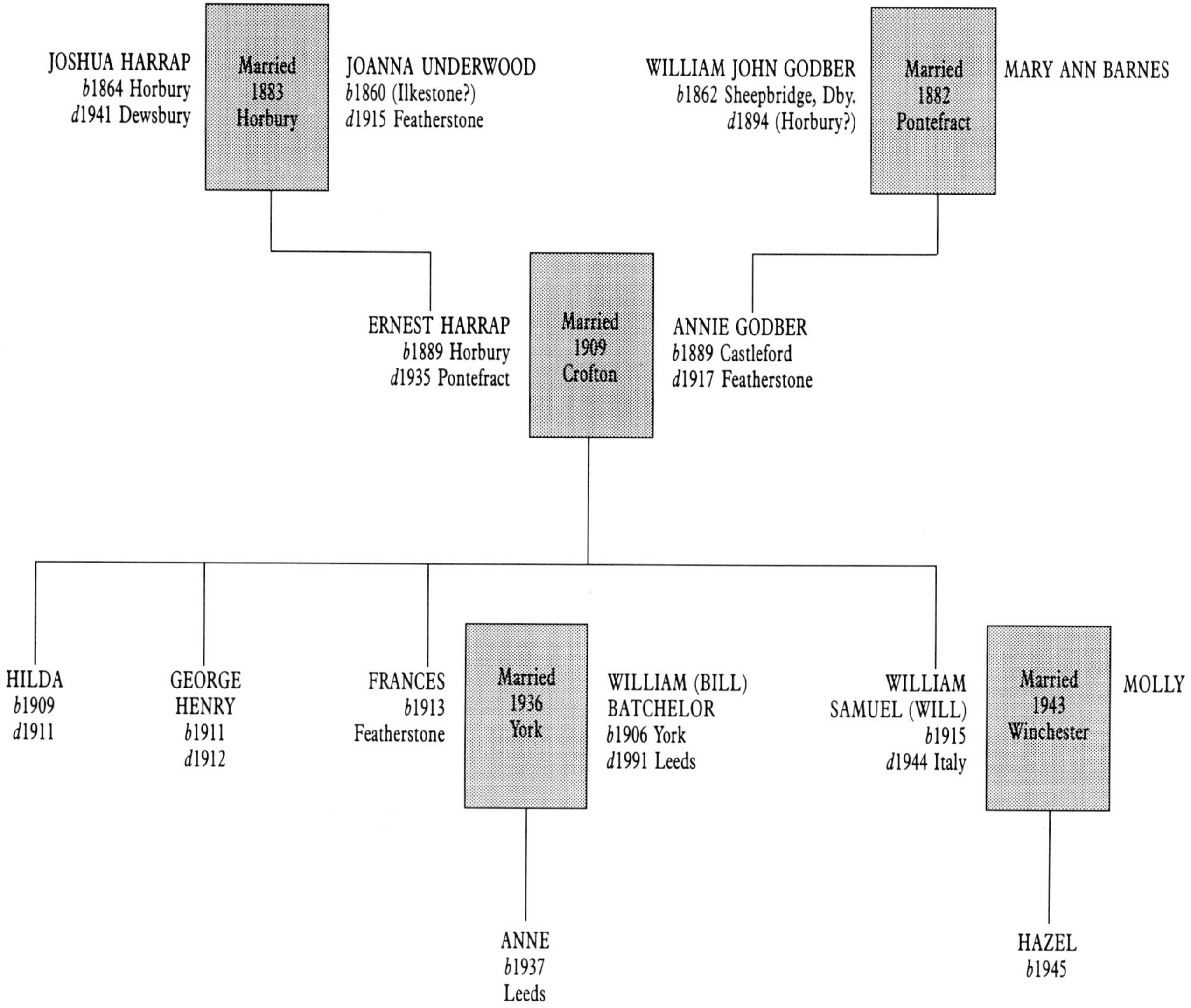
JOSHUA HARRAP
b1864 Horbury
d1941 Dewsbury
Married 1883 Horbury
JOANNA UNDERWOOD
b1860 (Ilkestone?)
d1915 Featherstone
WILLIAM JOHN GODBER
b1862 Sheepbridge, Dby.
d1894 (Horbury?)
Married 1882 Pontefract
MARY ANN BARNES
ERNEST HARRAP
b1889 Horbury
d1935 Pontefract
Married 1909 Crofton
ANNIE GODBER
b1889 Castleford
d1917 Featherstone
HILDA
b1909
d1911
GEORGE HENRY
b1911
d1912
FRANCES
b1913
Featherstone
Married 1936 York
WILLIAM (BILL) BATCHELOR
b1906 York
d1991 Leeds
WILLIAM SAMUEL (WILL)
b1915
d1944 Italy
Married 1943 Winchester
MOLLY
ANNE
b1937
Leeds
HAZEL
b1945

the doctor. We ran hand in hand, as fast as his little legs would go. I shall never forget it.'

I had always intended, one day, to research my mother's family story, while her memories were still clear and vivid. I decided that the time was right to begin my search. My knowledge of her family was very sparse. I knew that she had been born in Featherstone, West Yorkshire. I knew that she had a little sister, Hilda, who had died, aged two, of measles, and that her brother, Will, had grown up to become a boy-soldier in the band of the Royal Fusiliers, only to be killed in Italy in 1944. I knew, too, that on the death of her mother Mum was brought up in a Church of England Children's Home in York.

It was not a promising start to a genealogical quest but I am a profound optimist, with the unshakable belief that any family's story is somewhere 'out there' just waiting for the patient and persistent researcher to uncover it! So I set off on my search for my Harraps.

The first step was to gather together the certificates. Mum had her own birth and marriage certificates, but nothing more. So I spent many dusty hours in Leeds Reference Library, sifting through the St. Catherine's House Index of births, marriages and deaths to find what I needed. Around me I heard the subdued mutterings of family historians seeking their ancestors. 'Oh, come on, Fred, where *are* you? You must have been born *somewhere!*' As they say, this way madness lies!

I was lucky. Without too much seeking I found the marriage of my grandparents, Ernest and Annie, at a place called Crofton, near Wakefield. I then found Ernest's birth at Horbury, and the births of little Hilda and Will (William Samuel) at Featherstone. I found, too, the deaths of Hilda, Annie and Ernest. These certificates gave me addresses and somewhere to begin. The hunt was up!

I decided first to visit Crofton, where my grandfather, Ernest Harrap, had married Annie Godber in April 1909, when they were both just nineteen years old. I thought it would be a nice experience for Mum to visit the church where her parents were married, so off we went together. We had a lot of fun on the journey, getting lost and ending up in derelict colliery yards. In despair we stopped for refreshment at a typical miners' pub. Being a non-drinker I was never much of a pub-person before I took up family history, but they are a wonderful source of local knowledge as well as being an unofficial Tourist Information Bureau for lost travellers!

Eventually we entered Crofton village, to find the parish church perched on the top of a hill. Together Mum and I passed through the lych-gate and approached the massive church door – to find it locked! Will I never learn? I know that I should always write first to arrange access, but so many of my trips are spur of the moment

Ernest and Annie Harrap with little Hilda.

affairs that I just travel hopefully. Sadly there was no indication on the notice board of the location of the key, so we wandered around the churchyard, reading interesting tombstones. We didn't expect to find any of our Harraps there, of course, for this was not our village but simply the home church of Ernest's bride.

I do love reading old tombstones! They tell such stories and titillate the family historian with mysteries. I remember reading a stone at Wakefield Cathedral to Joze Luis Fernandes and wondering what he was doing in Wakefield at the beginning of the 19th century, so far from home. Poor chap, he and his wife, Martha, lost three little ones – Anthony aged one month, then Richard, two years two months, and then a daughter, Maria, aged sixteen weeks. How sad for poor Martha to carry them all the full nine months and then lose them so soon. Even across the centuries these stories touch us, for these are not just names carved in stone but real people.

And I wonder whatever happened to thirty-three year old James Pickles on 25 April, 1842? His tombstone at Wakefield reads:

> 'In evil long I took delight,
> Unaw'd by shame and fear,
> Till a new object struck my sight
> And stopped my wild career.'

The mind boggles! I suppose the only way I can discover what the 'new object' was would be to obtain James' death certificate. That would probably explain what hit him! You see how easily I get sidetracked and led astray, when I have plenty of mysteries and problems of my own to solve – but I just itch to know what happened to James.

The tombstones at Crofton made interesting reading, but we were interrupted by the arrival of a lady with a large shopping bag. We hoped that she was, perhaps, the church flower lady or cleaner, with a KEY! However, she passed the church door and continued down the path to the gate, obviously taking a short cut to the shops through the churchyard. She was our only hope, so I pounced on her.

I explained why I had brought my mother to Crofton church and asked where we might find someone with a key. She looked us up and down, and obviously decided that we were harmless. 'I know where there *is* a key,' she said, 'hidden in a secret place. If you both turn away for a moment and don't look, I'll get it for you.' Obediently we turned and admired the view, until she exclaimed, 'Here you are. I'll be back later so just leave it on the table inside.' So much for security! We could have done a runner with all the church valuables – had there been any! It is not unknown for thieves to steal the cross from off the altar. How low can people stoop?

However, Mum and I had no designs on the church plate. We were satisfied with just being there. We walked together up the aisle of the beautifully kept church and stood in silence before the altar. Then Mum said, 'Just think, my lovely red-haired mother stood here as a bride almost ninety years ago!' I could see that it was a moving moment so I didn't talk much. Instead I had a look at the church magazine on the table near the door.

I had a bright idea – I would write to the vicar, tell him of our visit and send a donation for some flowers in memory of the grandparents I had never known. I would ask him to mention in the service in whose name the flowers had been given. You never know, someone might be able to tell me something about Annie's family of Godbers. Never miss a trick – that's one of the secrets of successful family research! Sadly, on this occasion it drew a blank.

Now I needed to visit Featherstone, where Mum had been born and where so many of her family were buried. I decided to do a 'recce' myself first, to identify the places where my Harraps had lived, and then I would take Mum on a visit. I feel that it is important for her to be involved in my research as much as possible, for this is , after all, *her* story. My first port of call was to be the cemetery. Ernest, Annie and little Hilda are buried there, as are Ernest's parents, Joshua and Joanna Harrap, my great-grandparents.

My letter to the gatehouse was returned as 'Gone away', so I wrote to Pontefract Council asking whether they had any way of identifying my Harrap graves. I sent them one of my famous 'grovelling letters', guaranteed to get results! It began like this: 'Dear Sir or Madam, I know you must be *awfully* busy and letters like mine must be a great nuisance, but I would be so *very* grateful if you could possibly find the time, when you are not too busy, to help me.' It never fails – well, hardly ever!

By return post came a most helpful letter from a Mr. Leese of Wakefield Cemetery and Crematorium section of the Environmental Health Department. He sent a plan of the cemetery with my two Harrap graves marked, and a list of occupants. This revealed two surprising pieces of information. Firstly, little Hilda was not buried with her parents but across the path with Joshua and Joanna, her grandparents. This was probably because Ernest and Annie had no family grave yet.

In the same grave were two baby boys, both called George Henry Harrap. One of these, only eleven months old, had a birth date of 1911, which put him between little Hilda (1909) and my mother, Frances (1913). Was he perhaps a lost brother? Mum had no knowledge of him so I rang the number on Mr. Leese's letter and asked whether this child's parents were Joshua and Joanna, or Ernest and Annie.

'I'm sorry. I'm not allowed to say,' said the young man on the other end of the phone, 'but I am allowed to answer questions requiring only the answer "Yes" or "No". Would you like to rephrase your question and I'll see whether I can help.'

'Well,' said I, 'is that George Henry, born 1911, the son of Joshua and Joanna?'

'No,' said my young man. 'Ask me another.'

'Is he the son of Ernest and Annie then?'

'Yes!' he said with a note of triumph in his voice. 'Well done!'

What a carry on! I felt as though I had been competing in some crazy TV game show. At least I now had the truth – little Hilda was buried with her baby brother in their grandparents' grave. The other surprise in the burial record was that there was a baby in Ernest and Annie's grave, but it was not theirs. It was a nameless stillborn child 'of Reeves'. Alice Reeves was Ernest's niece. As she had at that time no family grave, she must have asked him to bury her tiny baby with his beloved Annie.

Now it was time for me to set off for Featherstone, to visit these almost unknown members of my maternal family. So one bright morning off I went, down the A1 with its thundering juggernauts, past Ferrybridge with its dramatic power station cooling towers, through the streets of Pontefract, and suddenly there was a road sign saying, 'Featherstone'. There is a strange magic about the moment when the place which was just a name on a document suddenly becomes a reality.

I called at a large pub at the top of Station Road for the usual sandwich and cuppa, and enquired the whereabouts of the cemetery. It couldn't have been easier. 'Just follow the road. You can't miss it.' Sure enough, there it was, right at the far end of the town, next to open fields of vivid yellow rape. A tree-lined avenue led from the empty gatehouse between rows of graves. The old graves were on the right and the modern ones on the left.

I was glad to see that the cemetery was still in use. It can be quite unnerving to walk around a derelict cemetery. Don't misunderstand me – I have no fear at all of the deceased. It is the glue sniffers and muggers who make cemeteries 'no-go areas' for the solitary visitor. Bring back the man in the gatehouse, that's what I say! Preferably with a large dog and a mobile phone, or perhaps CCTV.

A lady from my Family History class told me of an amusing incident concerning a man at a cemetery gatehouse. She had been helping her husband research his family and had managed to find Geoff's ancestor in a burial register. Together they had gone to the cemetery with some flowers, only to find that the plot number they had copied from the register was useless to them, for the rows of graves were unnumbered. Then they spotted an old chap in the gatehouse. They explained that they had brought flowers for Geoff's ancestor and asked whether he could help them find him. 'Oh aye,' said the old chap. 'Just wait a bit – Ah'll get mi spade!' As Ruth said, for one awful moment they thought they were going to see Geoff's long-dead ancestor face-to-face! However, the spade was only to flatten the nettles and brambles. What a shame!

Using my plan so thoughtfully provided by Wakefield Council I was able to find the spot where Ernest and Annie Harrap, the grandparents I never knew, were buried. It is a very special and personal moment to be in the presence of the mortal remains of one's ancestors. I felt sad that there was no stone marking their last resting place. Mum had remembered from long ago that originally it had a glass dome containing white china flowers, but they had long gone.

I decided that before I brought Mum I would arrange to have some kind of small stone put there, if I could afford it. I would have a word with my friend, Mr. Emmerson, the retired York stonemason who had restored my Batchelor grandparents' stone for me. As I retraced my steps to the cemetery gate, I remembered Mum telling me that when her father lost his job at the pit, due to an accident which took away half his heel, he was desperate for work and took a job as grave-digger at this very cemetery. It must have been a much pleasanter job, working here under the trees in the clean fresh air, than crawling about underground where it was always night.

The descriptions I had read of working conditions down the pit were chilling. No miner could stand erect to work and on some seams he could not even kneel in comfort. Sometimes only an inch or two separated the creaking roof from the miner's prostrate body as he crawled along. His food was eaten by the dim light of his safety lamp in the hot, stuffy, dust-laden and often gaseous atmosphere. At the end of his ten-hour working day he would walk, stoop or crawl back to the cage and the slow upward journey to the blessed fresh air. No wonder many miners suffered terrifying nightmares.

Unmarked but not forgotten.
Last resting place of Ernest and Annie.

Mother's Day 1997.

I was reminded of a folk song I once heard:

'It's as dark as a dungeon
And damp as the dew,
Where the dangers are many
And the pleasures are few,
Where the rain never falls
And the sun never shines -
It's as dark as a dungeon
Way down in the mines.'

I suppose the tough muscles he developed hacking away at the coal seams made my grandfather eminently suitable for digging out the soil for someone's grave.

For my next move in my exploration of my Featherstone roots, I drove back into the town with a list of addresses at which my family had lived. Amazingly, their birth, marriage and death certificates showed no fewer than ten addresses, the first eight of which covered just eight years. I really don't know why such a poor family would be constantly moving house. Presumably it was not because they owed rent, for their move from Allison Street to Henrietta Street only took them round the corner, where the landlord could easily track them down. Their other addresses, too, were within easy walking distance of each other. How strange.

Of course, moving house would not be the major operation it is today. Probably all their worldly possessions would fit on a cart. There would be no expensive fitted carpets to take up and refit – just a few home-made clip rugs. There would be no washing machine to unplumb – just a wooden peggy-stick, a wash-board and a tub to put on the cart. Life was much simpler, but far harder, for my grandmother. When I read a number of books on life in mining communities, the harsh reality of her life became clear to me.

Water came from a communal tap. She would have to queue up to fill her bucket and carry it back to her house. Lighting was by paraffin lamps or candles. The toilets

Henrietta Street, Featherstone

Remembrance Card for Annie Harrap

were dry closets with ash-pits at the back. Their smell was atrocious. In summer they were full of flies. In winter they were bitterly cold with a biting wind blowing up the lavatory seat. Brrrr! They were emptied by a muckman, who came with a horse and cart to carry away the evil-smelling contents. Ah, those were the good old days!

As the day was already wearing on, I decided to stop a while for refreshment. Not wanting to get a reputation for 'frequenting taverns' I found a modest but clean little café in the centre of the town. I ordered my pot of tea and a bacon sandwich (in memory of my Dad, who loved them!) and sat at a table by the window. At the next table sat a couple of old ladies who would have gladdened the heart of the writer, Alan Bennett. I'll bet my boots he gets all his brilliant dialogue from sitting in cafés and 'earwigging' on conversations as I was doing.

> 'Mornin', Elsie.'ow's yer lad nowadays?'
> 'Oh, ees champion now. Ees back at wuk termorrer. Docter sez it's a miracle after what ee's bin through.'
> 'Gerraway!'
> 'Aye, it's reet. 'Ow's yer old man? Arthur sed ee were off-colour.'
> 'Oh,'im – ee's'avin trouble wi''is watter-works agen.'
> 'Ne'mind, cock. Docter'll see'im reet. 'As 'e bin yet?'
> 'Nay,'e wain't go. Ye know men – daft about goin' t'Doctor's. Freetened what 'e might find!'
> 'Aye, men!!'

and they chuckled together. Then the old dears started to discuss their forthcoming holidays. I thought that they would be planning something like a week of Bingo at Bridlington – but no, one was heading for Bangkok! The other was returning for a fortnight to the Greek islands she had visited last year.

How times have changed. In my grandfather's day only the gentry would visit such exotic places. I'm afraid that in my old age I am becoming very patriotic. I have a passionate love for my own beautiful country and have no desire to travel anywhere else. With such loveliness as Cornwall in the Spring, the rugged East Yorkshire coast in the Summer and the Lake District in the Autumn, who needs 'abroad'? Not me!

Refreshed by my pot of good Yorkshire tea, I now set off to explore 'my Featherstone'. The idea was to photograph as many of our houses as I could. In Post Office Road, familiar to aficionados of Rugby League as the home ground of Featherstone RLC, I found number 67, the birthplace of little Hilda, and rang the bell. I don't feel that it is right or polite to just photograph someone's home without permission. After all, I could be a villain 'casing the joint' and planning to return at dead of night with a long ladder, a striped jersey and a bag marked, 'SWAG'!

Sadly, there was no-one at home at number 67, so I contented myself with studying the house from the other side of the road and comparing it with an old photograph I had of Olive Harrap, my grandfather's sister, standing at the gate around the year 1908. She wore button boots, a white pinafore and a ribbon in her hair. Although the house had been modernised, it was still possible to pick out the original structural features.

As I pondered over my photograph I was joined by a little lad who stood beside me for some time without speaking. He was obviously mystified by this strange woman staring across the road. I smiled and said, 'Hello,' and showed him my photograph. I told him that my great-grandfather, Joshua, had lived there almost a hundred years ago. He pointed across the road to the house next door to number 67 and said, 'That's where I live.' Then he studied the photograph closely and said, 'There's our house – look! But you can't see me on the picture!' I think he was quite disappointed. Obviously 'a hundred years ago' has no meaning to a small child.

Using my street map, bought from a friendly newsagent on Station Road, I then went looking for my mother's birthplace in Henrietta Street. Sadly, it no longer exists, except as a footpath behind a new development of rather grand modern houses. Henrietta Street, once known as 'Stewpot Row', used to face directly onto the pit slagheap belonging to Acton Hall Colliery, and families were constantly complaining about stones rolling down the heap and hitting their front doors. They couldn't have much of a view from their windows, either,

Olive Harrap outside 67 Post Office Road, Featherstone.

unlike Mum's wonderful view today, from the windows of her tenth-floor flat, right across the city of Leeds to the rolling hills of the distant Pennines and the Emley Moor mast.

Apparently the name, Stewpot Row, was given to the houses because the people there were so poor that they kept a stewpot on the hob all the time, eating a little every day and adding more of anything they could get, as and when they could get it. This information on old Featherstone was given to me by the prolific Featherstone writer, Tony Lumb. I read his books to gain some background knowledge of my mother's birthplace, wrote to him and found him to be a mine of information on the town, and so generous in the help he gives.

He helped me solve a couple of mysteries. Mum was born at 28, Henrietta Street, but the record of her baptism only a month later gives her address as '28, Englands Buildings'. I could find no trace of this address, but Tony told me that, at the turn of the century, small blocks of houses were sometimes known locally by the name of the builder or the owner. So perhaps Henrietta Street was built by, or for, a Mr. England.

The other question he was able to answer for me concerned Mum's eels! She has vivid memories of going, as a very small girl, with her father, at dead of night, to fish for eels. A good source of free food, I suppose, when times were hard. She remembers a group of men with lights – having to be very still and quiet – and eating the eels later, cooked in a large stewpot by one of the local women.

Tony wrote, 'Local people have heard of eel fishing by night. At that time the river Went, which rises in Streethouses, flowed past Featherstone and would be clean enough at the time to have eels. They could also have fished in Sharlston Dam, also not too far away. I have heard tales of such large catches that they would cook them in the kitchen set pot (or copper) and probably feed the whole street.' Nice to have Mum's memories confirmed like this!

Gradually I worked my way down the list of remaining Harrap addresses. Allison Street, where little George Henry had died, presented no problem. The street was still there – pity all the old houses had been demolished! Stanley Street, where he had been born a short eleven months earlier, was further to the north of the town. So also was Halton Street, birthplace of his brother, William Samuel. They were neat little back-to-back houses with no gardens, but with a view across open fields at the end of the road.

Duke Street, where both little Hilda and later her mother Annie had died, had vanished – or had it? There was still a short row of houses called *Back* Duke Street. Presumably if one went through the houses to their back doors one would be in (Front) Duke Street? A lady now living in Back Duke Street was most insistent about it not being the original street, but I have my doubts!

Before I went home, at the end of a very long day, I visited St. Thomas' Parish Church, where my mother was christened in 1913. The vicar obviously thought I looked too honest to run off with the church plate, so he lent me the key to let myself in. Perhaps he also noticed my swollen feet, which I call 'mumps of the feet'! After pounding the streets of Featherstone all day I would hardly be able to run far if I *did* have designs on his treasures!

I stood beside the stone font and imagined Ernest and his red-haired wife presenting little Frances for baptism, fervently praying that this child would survive longer than Hilda and George Henry. I feel sure that it would please them to know that she is already in her eighties!

As for marking their last resting place, I could not afford to pay for a full size gravestone, but my good friends at Emmerson's Stonemasons at York Cemetery made a lovely flower container for their grave – a large cube of white marble which was inscribed with their

names and dates, along with those of little Hilda, and my words, 'NOT FORGOTTEN'. I do think that is very important. After all, I owe my very existence to those ancestors of mine. I see it as my duty to see that they are remembered.

When I eventually brought Mum on a visit, with a lovely bunch of spring flowers, it was Mothers' Day. I felt it was a fitting day on which to visit her mother. 'Poor Mam and Dad,' she said. 'They didn't have much of a life. At least they will be remembered now.'

Before we went home I drove her to Regent Street School. A few weeks earlier I had worked my way through a heap of old Featherstone school registers at Wakefield Archives and had found 'Frances Harrap' on the register of Regent Street. The school still stands between Regent Street and Post Office Road, but now it is used as a resource centre rather than a school. Mum studied it for a few moments and said, 'No, I don't really recognise it. I was only six when I left Featherstone, remember. But I do remember Empire Day. We all had to salute the flag and march round the playground.' In my mind's eye I imagined all those little children – the girls in their white pinnies and the boys in short trousers – heads up, arms swinging, marching stiff-legged in celebration of the Empire. How times have changed.

I had studied the school log books at Wakefield in the hope of finding some mention of my little Frances, but without success. Log books can provide a wonderful picture of school life. I can never resist scribbling down interesting entries, even when they have nothing at all to do with my family! For instance:

NEWBOLD SCHOOL, DERBYSHIRE

March, 1868 – Complaint from Mrs. Clarke of some children knocking on her door and annoying her dog.

November, 1868 – Sent Sarah Henry home for coming to school in a filthy, dirty state. Her mother is very angry and refuses to let her come to school again.

March, 1869 – The pupil teacher is saucy and would rather play marbles with the boys in the playground than work.

What fun it would be to discover what happened to that 'saucy' teacher in later life!

Now I set myself the task of uncovering the story of my mother's days in the York children's home where she grew up. I wrote for information to the York City Archives, but sadly they had no records of the Godfrey Walker Home at Acomb. Neither had York Reference Library, but they *were* able to send me some newspaper cuttings about the opening of the Home in 1911.

Mum remembered that it had been a Church of England Home, so I wrote to the Church of England's Children's Society to see whether they had any records of their Home at York. Their reply plunged me into the depths of despair. 'Almost no records of the Godfrey Walker Home have survived.' Then the Archivist, Ian Wakeling, remarked, quite casually, 'I have, however, been able to locate your mother's case-file.' Bless the man! This was the most thrilling news. How amazing that, after more than seventy-five years, her personal file had survived. What might this file reveal about her early years, I wondered.

I requested photocopies of every item in the file, sent a large donation which would more than cover the cost, and sat chewing my nails for what felt like years. I could be seen regularly accosting my postie, Simon, in the street and pleading, with outstretched hands, for anything in a large brown envelope. At last it arrived – large and heavy and wonderful! It contained copies of all the official documents relating to Mum's entry into the care of the society, then called 'The Waifs and Strays Society', in 1920, plus numerous letters about her and details of her placement in work ten years later.

What was such a surprise to me was the detail which was revealed of the circumstances in which she entered the Home. I had always imagined her recently widowed father going to the vicar and saying, 'Can you get my children placed in a Home? I can't manage to look after them myself.' The file revealed that this was not how it happened at all.

The first document in the file was signed by a Sister E. J. Tomlinson of 'The Haven', Pontefract. She was applying to Edward Rudolf, the actual founder of the Waifs and Strays Society, on behalf of my grandfather. This was very exciting for me – rather like having a personal link with Dr. Barnardo!

She wrote:

> 'Dear Sir,
>
> Could you, if you have two vacancies in one of your homes, take two children, a boy and a girl. The girl is 7 years next April and the boy 5 years in April. Their mother died two years ago and it is very difficult for their father, who is away at work in the daytime, to bring them up in a proper way. He came to us in distress telling us that he is in lodgings and the two children; the landlady will not have them longer than the 17th of this month. He would rather that they were brought up in a Home, where they would be brought up properly, he says. The locality in which they live is very immoral, but the man's works is there. He would be able to pay for them. Will you kindly send forms –'

The accompanying form shows that Ernest tried for two years to keep his precious children, his living link with his beloved Annie. For the first year they all lived with his parents in Post Office Road, but Joshua and Joanna Harrap had a large family of their own and Joshua was too sick to work. He was described by Sister Tomlinson as, '– almost an invalid who has not worked for 18 months.' They must have found it difficult to cope, in their small house, with their own large family plus another adult and two extra children.

So Ernest found lodgings in Rhyll Street with a landlady, the widow of his friend who had died in a pit accident. She looked after the children when he was at work. Mum vaguely remembers her time there. 'I was five then. I had a bit of a temper and she used to put my head under the cold tap to cool me down!' She remembers, too, falling out with her little brother, Will, because he took her 'treasure'. It was an empty talcum powder tin which someone had given her. She liked it because of the nice smell. Poor little Frances! When I think about children of today with their computer games and mountain bikes I realise how times have changed. They feel badly done by if they don't have the right kind of trainers or designer jeans. They don't know they are born!

Then came the awful day when the Rhyll Street landlady said, 'Enough!' Probably she found the care of the two little children very restricting. So she gave my grandfather the awful ultimatum – 'You have until the 17th to get rid of them.' What was he to do? Where could he take his motherless children? He had managed to keep his little family together for two years, but what was to become of them now?

Then he remembered Sister Tomlinson and Sister Weaving, at the mother and baby home in Pontefract. They had taken in his young sister when she was 'in trouble' and had helped his family again by placing another sister in service. So he turned to them.

On the application form which Sister Tomlinson submitted to the Waifs and Strays Society, she describes again how he came 'in distress' and begged her to take them in, and find them a place in a Home. She adds, 'He is a very respectable man, but Featherstone is a most immoral place. The reason that I think they should be away is because they have not a mother's care.'

My poor grandfather. I must admit I shed tears for him when I discovered this story. He had lost his first child, little Hilda; then his first son, the infant George Henry; then his beloved wife, and now he had to give away his two precious children, Frances and Will. The obvious solution, of course, would have been to remarry and provide the children with a new mother, but Mum says that he had promised Annie, on her deathbed, that he would never take another wife.

Frances and Will stayed at The Haven for a month, while the Waifs and Strays Society deliberated on their application. In her written record of her memories, Mum writes,

> 'I don't remember much about the Home at Pontefract, only that when we went to church we were given a picture-book. We were told to keep quiet and look at the pictures of Jesus.'

Someone who came to visit The Haven, perhaps looking for a baby to adopt, offered to adopt four-year old Will, who was a sweet-faced, fair-haired boy. However, his father would not agree unless they took Frances as well. He said that he did not want them to have different surnames – he wanted Will always to know that he had a sister. Sadly, the couple were not prepared to take both children. I can't help wondering how different their lives might have been if they had been adopted. We shall never know.

Meanwhile Sister Tomlinson continued to natter the Waifs and Strays Society, for her refuge was getting overcrowded. As a general rule the Society did not take in children with a living parent, but eventually they decided to take the Harrap children. Ernest now had to sign the fateful document, giving away all his rights to his children. He signs in a clear, firm hand but as he did so his heart must have been well nigh breaking. He must have wondered whether he was doing the right thing for his children. I wish there was some way of letting him know now that he made the right decision.

> 'I, Ernest Harrap, of 11, Rhyll Street, Featherstone, parent of Frances, do hereby commit her wholly to the care of the Society, and promise to obey the rules in force, to permit the said child to be brought up in the faith of the Church of England, and when fully trained to be sent to any situation in the United Kingdom which may be obtained for her by the committee.'

He also signed an agreement to pay 'the sum of twelve shillings per week towards the maintenance of Frances and Willie Harrap my children while they remain under the care of the above Society.' This was a very large payment out of his weekly wage of £1 17s. 6d. (i.e. £1.88). He paid 12s. to the Society, his board and lodgings, 1s. 9d to his union and 2s. insurance. This left very little money for such luxuries as beer, baccy or boots! I was very touched to read that he offered to take a collecting tin around the miners to raise money for the Society.

Life continued to deal heavy blows on my poor grandfather. An accident at the pit left him with a damaged heel and he had to leave. He went to live with his brother and got the grave digging job at the cemetery. However, his brother, who was out of work, was told that he would lose his dole money if Ernest, a wage-earner, lived in the same house. So my grandfather moved into lodgings with a very nice Salvation Army family. These were the depression years and jobs were scarce – so his job at the cemetery was taken from him and given to a man who had a family to feed. Mum says that it broke his heart to become unemployed. It took away his personal dignity.

He must have been a remarkable man, for, in spite of all that life threw at him, he continued to smile and joke. An example – Frances to her father when he had several teeth removed, 'You ought to get some false teeth. Then you might get off with someone!' 'Off what?' said her father. 'Off a bus?' Not screamingly funny, I know, but a sign of the wonderful spirit which kept him going through all the troubles he had seen. This was the same spirit which carried Frances through those traumatic early days and earned her the nickname of 'Smiler'. Likewise her brother Will was remembered in later years for his infectious laughter. Perhaps this is where I get *my* daft sense of humour! I would like to think so.

I have tried to discover more about dear Sister Tomlinson of The Haven, but with little success. I did find a lady in Wetherby, Jean Garside, who knew a Tomlinson family in Pontefract in the 1920s. The son, Tom, was a headmaster, Amelia (Mamie) was a teacher, and Lilian '– was rather like a District Nurse – she worked in a 'Babies Welcome' clinic.' Could she be my Sister Tomlinson? My lady signs herself clearly as 'E.J.' on all her letters about the Harrap children, not L. for Lilian. Perhaps she was another daughter of Mrs. Tomlinson. Or perhaps she had a pet name as Amelia had. Could she perhaps be Elizabeth – known as Lily – then as Lilian? After all, our present queen was known as 'Lilibet' as a child. Maybe one day I shall discover the answer.

I feel that I owe such a debt of gratitude to Sister Tomlinson, God bless her. If she had turned my grandfather away because The Haven was only for mothers and newborn babies, not motherless six-year-olds, as she had every right to do, then who knows what might have become of my little mother in that 'most immoral place' of Featherstone? She certainly would never have grown up in York, would never have met and married my father there, and I would not exist as me! It is a sobering thought, which is why I pour blessings on the head of Sister E. J. Tomlinson, whoever she was.

At last, after much deliberation, the Waifs and Strays Society found places for Frances and little Will. It was decided that Frances would be admitted into St. Christopher's Home, Balby, near Doncaster – only to be altered a week later to – 'our Godfrey Walker Home at York.' Phew! That was a near thing, Dad! Once again her path of life almost led her away from York. As for little 'Willie' Harrap, her brother, it was to be another year before I managed to uncover the story of his fate.

Dear Sister Tomlinson, concerned to the last with her charge, personally took Frances to York. So it was that, on 21 February, 1920, she left the town of her birth, leaving behind her loving father, her grandparents, her little brother – in fact everyone that she knew – and was handed over to the Matron of the Godfrey Walker Home for Girls. As she crossed the threshold of the small terrace house in the Holgate district of York, which was to be her home for the next ten years, little six-year-old Frances was completely alone.

Featherstone Cemetery.

CHAPTER TWO

ONE OF THE 'HOME GIRLS'

It was Mother's Day, 1996. Frances, now an eighty-two-year-old widow, struggled up the steps and reached the door of 4, West Bank Terrace. I stood back, to let her open it herself. 'This is your special moment,' I said. The heavy door opened easily and Mum stepped across the threshold of the house which had been the Godfrey Walker Home in the 1920s. This was her homecoming after almost seventy years.

Her memories of those early days were still vivid in her

Godfrey Walker Home – end house, West Bank Terrace, York.

Return to Godfrey Walker Home.

mind, and came tumbling out. 'That's Matron's room, there at the back, and this big front room was the living room where we played. I remember, someone gave us a wind-up gramophone with a big horn and one record – a march. I think it was *Stars and Stripes*. We used to play it over and over again, and march round the room swinging our arms. I think Matron must have been relieved when we finally wore it out!'

From outside the building, now converted into private flats, she could identify every room. 'There, in the basement, was the dining-room. There was a shoe-rack just inside the door, where we came in from school. We put our shoes there. When it was your birthday you could invite a friend to tea and you sat at a special table. You felt very grand! That large bay-window belonged to the living room. Above that were the bedrooms – the 'Five Room' and the 'Nine Room'. Above them, on the next floor, was the 'Six Room' for the six oldest girls.

Next to that was the sick bay. I hated being in there. There was a door leading to the fire-escape, and I used to lie in bed staring at it. I thought someone would come in after dark and get me!' She remembered that, in one of the rooms, there was a 'secret cupboard'. Only the big girls knew what it contained. When Mum was old enough she was allowed to open the secret cupboard, which contained – sanitary towels! What a disappointment. She felt sure it would contain something wonderful!

'We had lumpy porridge for breakfast,' she told me. 'It often made me sick. Sometimes we had dripping and bread. The dripping was collected in a large basin from the kitchen door of the Royal Station Hotel and brought home on the tram.' Little did she know that her husband-to-be was working as a young cellar-man in that same hotel. Nor did she imagine that one day, as an old lady, she would be staying in that very grand hotel for a short holiday!

She remembered having an egg *once a year*, at Easter. What a luxury! Then – confession time – she told me that someone once gave the Home a large tin of solid white honey, and little Frances used to tiptoe into the kitchen and sneak a spoonful! Then she remembered her broken suspender. It was Sunday, but she couldn't go to church, for sewing was forbidden on the Sabbath. Looking up at the bedroom windows, she remembered watching the last tram going to Acomb terminus every night, the lights moving slowly across the ceiling of the bedroom.

So many memories, and so vivid. She was visibly moved as they all came flooding back. 'When I lived here,' she said, 'I never thought that one day I would be standing here with a daughter of my own.' When we got home I gave her a large foolscap notebook in which she could write down some of her memories. Now, whenever she says, 'I remember when —' I thrust a pen in her hand and say, '*Write it down!*' Many parts of this book are based on what she wrote for me in her memory notebook.

I asked her one day what she remembered about the day she arrived at Godfrey Walker. 'I don't remember that day,' she said, 'but I must have been quite scared when Sister Tomlinson left me with Matron and Sister. They wore long black habits, like nuns. There were twenty girls in the Home. Matron was like the house-mother and Sister was in charge of medical matters. I remember a rather grand lady coming to visit us and giving us each a wicker basket to keep our clothes in under the bed, and a small square of carpet to put beside each bed.'

What a luxury that must have been. Probably the floor was covered with oilcloth – very cold for little feet on cold winter mornings! How they must have blessed her thoughtfulness and generosity. When I visited the Archives of the Children's Society in London and read through some early Waifs and Strays magazines, I noticed the report of a visit by a 'Mrs. Geoffrey Walker of Scarborough and Exeter'. She was the person who donated the Home in 1911, in memory of her son, Godfrey. She had visited the Home in February, 1924, to see what the girls needed. Some time later she returned and her visit was reported in the magazine:

> 'YORK – From here comes a tale of a fairy god-mother who has recently visited the Home and presented a blanket and a strip of carpet to each bed, furnished the sick room, supplied special pillows and sheets, furnished a first-aid cupboard, promised mackintosh capes for each child, and supplied a carpet and hearthrug for Matron's room. The Honorary Secretary says, "The children are enchanted, and so are we all".'

Bless the lady, she would be very surprised to know that her kindness is still remembered over seventy years later by one of the children. I thought it would be interesting to find some living descendant of this Walker family. Perhaps they might have photographs of the inside of the Home. As she was described as being '– of Scarborough and Exeter', I sent cries for help to newspapers in both places. 'Dear Editor, I know you must be awfully busy –'. I never worry about knowing the name of the newspaper or its exact address. I trust my wonderful friends in Royal Mail. I simply address my envelope to '- The Editor, The largest local newspaper in Scarborough (or Exeter), Scarborough, YO1 (or Exeter, EX1).' I put a first class stamp on the envelope to show I mean business, and trustingly drop it in the postbox.

It never fails – well, hardly ever. We have the best postal system, and the best posties, in the world! Both editors published my small article, accompanied by a photograph of two smiling Batchelors – to give the enquiry a human face. Sadly there was no response and I never did make contact with any descendants of kind Mrs. Walker.

Mum still remembers, when she was very young, sleeping in a cot which had a brass plate suspended from the metal bars of the bed-head. The plate bore the name of 'Godfrey Walker'. The cot was too small for her long legs, and the plate rattled whenever she moved about or turned over. 'It rang and rang, and kept me awake,' she told me. 'I really *hated* that cot.'

Those old Waifs and Strays magazines made fascinating reading. There were some heart-rending stories in the section headed, 'Will you be my friend?' Here the society was appealing for sponsors who would pay £30 p.a. to support a child. For instance, there was 'Charles W.G. aged 7. His father is paralysed and his mother, it is said, looks the picture of starvation. There are four other children, and Charles is described as a dear, intelligent little boy. Will some friend of the Society give this little fellow a chance in life?'

Another needy child was Winifred E. aged 11. 'Father unknown, mother presumed living but cannot be traced. No brothers or sisters. She has previously been kept in a House of Compassion. Will someone now befriend this lonely child?' Poor sad little Winifred. I can't help wondering what became of her. I do hope she found love and happiness.

Turning from these touching stories, I had a quiet grin to myself over the titles of two articles. 'A Bachelor Among the Babies,' said one, and 'Bachelors Befriend Bonny Babies,' said another. Not a reference to my family, alas, but to the support given to the Society by elderly unmarried gentlemen!

I combed the magazines for some mention of the Godfrey Walker Home in the years that my mother was there, and came up with this:

> '*June, 1922* – Wanted in the Godfrey Walker Home – serge, underclothing and stockings, old and new.
> *September, 1922* – Wanted – navy cotton knickers, woollen vests, stockings and tea-cloths.
> *February, 1924* – Wanted – Muslin for curtains, bath towels, overalls for girls of all ages and brown knickers for quite small girls.'

Nice to think that my eight-year-old Mum probably wore those navy knickers, a woollen vest and stockings in 1922! I do know what size she wore, for her personal case-file at The Children's Society contains a wealth of information on her. When she entered Godfrey Walker at the age of six, her height was 4ft. (quite tall, hence the problem with the cot!), but her weight was only 3 st. 8 lb. and her chest measurement ('in nipple line with lungs moderately inflated'!) was only 22 ins. I got out a tape-measure and made a circle of 22 ins. It was tiny. Now, when I look at my eighty-four-year old mother, I see, in my mind's eye, this little golden-haired child with the skinny ribs!

In the magazine for August, 1927, I came across a mention of the Matron my mother remembers best. Mabel Wood gave a talk describing the work in a Home, to Newton-on-Ouse Garden Meeting. That was followed by an 'American Tea'. I would love to know what that was. Certainly not a Macdonald's and Coke! Perhaps it was that universal cream tea which crops up wherever you take your holiday. Known as a 'Devon Tea' in Ilfracombe, a 'Cornish Tea' in Newquay, a 'Yorkshire Tea' in Haworth and a 'Derbyshire Tea' in Matlock – all identical scones, cream and jam! Probably, when we have colonised the moon, holidaymakers there will be offered 'Lunar Cream Teas'! After Mabel Wood's American Tea, there was a collection for the work of the Waifs and Strays Society which raised £9

My favourite story from the Society concerns a twin brother and sister, cared for in one of their Homes. They were adopted as babies by a childless couple who explained to them, as soon as they were old enough to understand, that they had been living in a house full of babies and that their adoptive parents had been to the house and chosen them for their own. The little boy in particular was fascinated by the idea of a house full of babies, and constantly nattered to be taken to visit it. He was about six when he and his sister finally went back. After a tour of the house the little fellow remarked to the Matron, 'When I grow up, I should like to have a baby. Will you save one for me?' His little sister, however, had other ideas. 'Not for me,' she said. 'When I grow up I'm going to make my *own* babies!' I can't help wondering what did happen when they grew up. I wonder how many of her own babies she made!

It was at the Godfrey Walker Home that Frances became 'Joan', and later 'Fanny'. When she went to school at St. Paul's, Holgate Road, she was known as '– one of the Home girls'. It is quite remarkable that she managed to keep her sense of identity under these circumstances. That was due, I'm sure, to the fact that her father kept in touch with her, and visited her when his work (and his financial situation) allowed. She remembers that, when he lodged with a Salvation Army family, his landlady used to make pikelets in her copper, and always sent him to visit his daughter with a parcel of this Yorkshire teacake in his pocket for all the little girls.

She also remembers her great distress as she waited one day for his visit – and he never arrived. She sat all day in the big bay-window, looking out for him. The date was somewhere between 4-12 May, 1926. She had no way of knowing that the whole of England had been paralysed by a General Strike in which six million Trade Union members, all over the country, had downed tools in support of the miners. No trains, buses or trams were running on that day as she sat crying in the window.

Sometimes, as a special treat, she went to Featherstone to visit her father. She would be put on a train in York, in the care of the guard, who was instructed to put her off at Featherstone Station where her father would be waiting to meet her. On one never-to-be forgotten occasion, as the train drew into *Pontefract* Station, she told the guard, 'This is where I live.' She was so insistent that he, rather reluctantly, put her off the train. Could she, I wonder, have had some faint memory of catching the York train at Pontefract with Sister Tomlinson many years before? Or perhaps it was just the name which rang a distant bell?

Of course, having got her own way and having been put off the train, there was no-one there to meet her! Meanwhile the train puffed off to Featherstone where her father was waiting for her. Imagine his consternation when the train disgorged its passengers and there was no little Frances. She, of course, was at Pontefract, sitting on the base of a large weighing machine – 'Your weight for a penny' – and sobbing her heart out!

A concerned porter questioned her and decided to help her. Taking her by the hand, he led her along the street outside the station, asking everyone he met, 'Do you recognise this little girl?' You would not dare do such a thing in these wicked times. Amazingly, someone eventually recognised the little girl with the striking golden hair and said, 'Oh, she's from The Haven.'

The porter led her back to the Mother and Baby Home and dear Sister Tomlinson. Mum still remembers being given a large mug of cocoa whilst someone telephoned Featherstone Station to tell the distraught Ernest Harrap that his precious lost daughter was safe. 'It was kind of them,' she writes in her notebook, 'but it was right bitter! I still remember the taste of that cocoa. Ugh!'

I can imagine what my grandfather must have said to her when he eventually arrived on the next Featherstone/ Pontefract train! Probably, whenever she repeated this journey, they stuck a label on her coat saying, 'Deliver to Featherstone Station and *nowhere else!*'

Life was not so bad at the Godfrey Walker Home. The girls were fed, clothed and cared for. The successive Matrons and Sisters were kind but not affectionate to individual children. They were not allowed to be, for that might promote jealousy. So there were no hugs or kisses throughout Frances's childhood.

The girls had their own Brownies and Guides – an open company so that other girls from outside the Home could join, too. There was Guide camp, and lots of singing. Mum told me that one year they won a singing competition, and in *Our Waifs and Strays Magazine, 1923*, I was thrilled to find the following –

York Home Guides, April 1923.
Frances as a Brownie, front row, second from left.

> 'YORK – The Home Guides took part with twenty-three other companies in the Folk Singing Contest on May 4th, at the Festival Concert Rooms, and gained the highest marks. The two songs they gave were, "I'm Seventeen come Sunday" and (their own choice) "The Cuckoo".'

Ian Wakeling, the excellent Archivist at the Children's Society, sent me a photograph, from the magazine, of 'York Home Guides, April 1923.' I started to run my eye along the rows of faces, but Mum beat me to it. 'That's me,' she said, hardly able to disguise the excitement in her voice, 'on the front row, as a Brownie.' Sure enough, there was little Frances, aged almost ten, wearing her brown knitted Brownie hat and smiling at the camera.

A number of other group photographs yielded pictures of her. October 1921 – 'That's me on the right with the big ribbon in my hair, and that's the dolly they gave me for being a good girl.' September 1922 – 'I'm on the front row, in the white dress. The girl behind me, on Matron's knee, is the other Frances, who took my name. She was Frances Davenport.' October 1927 – 'I'm the tall girl at the back, smiling.' In fact, on all those photographs can be seen the same bright smile she has today, seventy years later.

After all this time she can still put names to some of the other faces. 'Sarah Price – and her sister, Mary. That's Anita something. There's the girl who became a teacher – we were all very proud of her. And that's the girl who was burnt to death.'

Mum remembers this horrific incident vividly. 'We did the washing in a big set-pot in a small brick building in the back yard. There was a fire under the pot to heat the water. You had to wear a hessian pinny to protect you from the sparks. One day this girl didn't put her pinny on. She was raking the fire under the pot when a spark flew out and set fire to her clothes. I can still hear her screams! People rushed to help but it was too late and she died. We all tip-toed about and spoke in whispers for the rest of that day. I suppose we were in a state of shock.'

All the group photographs in the magazine were taken on the annual holiday in Filey. If Frances had remained in Featherstone with her father, I doubt whether she would ever have had a sea-side holiday. The Home girls were taken every year. Often a report of the holiday appeared in the *Waifs and Strays Magazine.*

> 'October 1926 – 'I am writing to tell you how we enjoyed our summer holiday. The very first thing we did when we reached our wooden hut was to fill our mattresses with straw, which was great fun. A day or two after, we had some competitions, and we did animals, houses and gardens. One day we went to Filey Brigg and went winkling, and we took them home and had them for dinner. We have had several

competitions, one of which is pressed flowers, and the first prize is two shillings. We have been to St. John's Church twice, St. Oswald's once, and yesterday we walked to Hunmanby to All Saints' Church. We are all very sorry indeed to come back but we must go. The birds are beautiful here. I hope you had a nice holiday like us.' ROSE E. H.

(Mum thinks this was Rose Harland)

October 1929 – 'Our holiday again at Filey this year has been most ripping! except for the weather being uncertain. We were all excited to go but very sorry to come back. While we were playing on the sands, we made friends with the Darlington Home, where the girls are very jolly. We bathed every morning possible, and we had such grand times in the sea, especially our tiny baby Doreen. One day some of the elder girls went winkling to Filey Brigg but, worst luck, they came back with only seven winkles, saying that they must have gone out to tea!' JESSIE

The Home girls were at the receiving end of a great deal of kindness. Because their Brown Owl was the daughter of the Lord Mayor of York, the girls were invited to tea at the Mansion House at Christmas. I can visualise the twenty little girls gazing, wide-eyed, at the chandeliers and fine paintings. A far cry indeed from Henrietta Street, Featherstone. Another Christmas '– much pleasure has been given to all at the Godfrey Walker Home by the very kind gift of a delightful wireless set with loudspeaker, from their parish church, St. Paul's. So that they should have their share in the gift, a number of the young people of the church went carol-singing and gave the result of their efforts in this way towards the cost of the wireless set.'

I took a trip, one day, to the York City Archives, hidden away behind the Art Gallery, to see the St. Paul's School log books, hoping that the name of Frances Harrap might appear in them. No such luck, but I did find this:

> '21 April, 1920 – School opened at 1 o'clock and closed at 3 o'clock, to enable the children from the Godfrey Walker Home to go out to tea.'

Mum remembers meeting the famous 'Walking Parson' of Filey, and watching pierrots on the beach. She sometimes quotes one of their songs to me – 'There's nothing wrong with the world, it's the people that are in it!' On seeing the sea for the first time, she exclaimed, 'Oh – what a *big* bath!' I suppose it was an amazing sight to someone from land-locked Featherstone.

Godfrey Walker Girls at Filey c1921. Frances front row, second from left.

'3 August 1922 – The Home Girls have been invited to Askham Bryan Hall.'

Mum remembers this visit. 'Lady Payne-Galloway sent her big black Daimler to collect us. We all packed in – twenty of us! I had to sit on the floor, so I couldn't see out of the window. We were all in a heap.' When they opened the doors it must have looked like one of those 'How many people can you fit inside a 'phonebox?' events which were popular in the 1960s!

The girls were given tea in the house, waited on by maids. What a wonderful experience for Home Girls! Then they were taken into the garden. Frances thought this was amazing. There had been no garden at her Featherstone home. At Godfrey Walker there was just a tiny patch of garden which she helped to tend. Here at Askham Bryan was a garden so huge you could walk around in it, and the roses were spectacular.

Lady Payne-Galloway must have noticed her delight, for she picked a bunch of flowers and put them into her hands. It was a small, spontaneous gesture of generosity towards a nine-year-old child which has never been forgotten.

Another kind friend of the Home Girls was Christina Jessie Paget, Honorary Secretary to the Home for fifteen years. Her obituary describes her as – 'Beloved by all who knew her. She gave of her time freely for the benefit of the children in the Home, and did all that she could for their comfort and happiness.'

Then there was their neighbour, Colonel Birks. He lived in West Garth, a very grand house in its own grounds. Mum remembers how he used to invite the girls and staff to tea, where they were waited on by his manservant – probably his batman from his army days. He often invited them in, too, for Christmas dinner. I suppose, as an old bachelor, it was nice to have an adopted family.

When he died the house was put up for sale and it was eventually bought by the Society for the girls of the Godfrey Walker Home. When large children's Homes went out of fashion, they sold it in 1981 for £80,000. The local press gave an impressive description of it:

> 'Standing in twelve acres of grounds in Acomb, the house, built at the turn of the century, has ten bedrooms, three reception rooms, and four bathrooms. A five-roomed coach-house and three-bedroomed bungalow also stand on the site.'

How different life must have been for the Home Girls when they moved from a small terrace house into such grand surroundings.

West Garth is now an excellent hotel called The Carlton and I took Mum there for a Mother's Day Sunday lunch. I was curious to see what she would remember of her visits to the house in Col. Birks' days. I thought she might remember the fine staircase, but there was no response. However, in the dining-room she suddenly said, 'I recognise that fireplace. It used to have a collection of shells on it.' I thought that she meant seaside

Godfrey Walker Home, West Garth, Acomb Road, York. 1952

shells, but she corrected me. 'No, shells from big guns.' Strange the way our memory selects what to retain and what to forget. I thought that she would remember the grand house, with its huge mirrors and paintings. Instead she remembers the old military gentleman entertaining the girls with exciting tales from the war.

I do feel that my mother was lucky to find a place in a church-run Home. Edward Rudolf, the Society's founder, had been so touched by the plight of the children in his Sunday School classes that he put his faith into action by providing a home for the most needy and troubled. God bless him for that! So the Waifs and Strays Society grew directly from the church.

The Godfrey Walker Home was opened in 1911 by the Archbishop of York, assisted by Edward Rudolf himself. The Archbishop's words, which I found in a newspaper report of the event, sum up the philosophy behind the Society:

Edward Rudolf, God bless him!

> 'He liked to think that the special method they had established in their church of dealing with their children was not to bring them into great institutions; but to do everything they could to prevent anything that suggested the "institution" surrounding the lives of the children. The plan of the church was to make the children feel that their mother Church wished them to realise they were members of a family living in a home. He prayed God's richest blessing might rest upon those who would do the work there, and upon the children –'

Now I thought it would be nice to find one of the Home Girls so that Mum could swop stories and memories, but that proved to be more difficult than I had expected. True, my mother's contemporaries will all be old ladies now, but I would have thought that some of them would have survived. I put a notice in the *Yorkshire Evening Press*, and on Channel 4's *Lost Touch* service on Teletext, asking for any old girl from Godfrey Walker, 1920s, to get in touch with me.

I had just one reply, from a lady called Mary, who lived in Easingwold, a village to the north of York. She wrote:

> 'At that time I attended St. Paul's School, Holgate Road, York, and the children from the Home were also pupils. It seems quite a coincidence that two names I can remember most are Frances Harrap and Dorothy Harland. Dorothy would be more my age – I am now 83. I may be wrong but my memories of Frances were she was a slim girl with very pretty hair.'
>
> Mary Willis (née Dearlove)

How amazing! Mum did not recognise the name, but when I wrote back to Mary she invited us to visit her and her husband, and have tea with them. After a short drive from Leeds we found Easingwold and were met with open arms and hugs from Mary. It was a very lovely moment for Mum to come face to face with someone from her past. It was only the first of such adventures Mum was to have and, as such, will always have a special place in our memories.

As soon as they met, the memories of their school-days

came flooding back and the two elderly ladies, both in their eighties, suddenly became young again. 'Do you remember Miss Moss, the Headteacher? Wasn't she strict!' they giggled. 'And there was Miss Lord – and Mrs. Robinson.'

Mum told Mary of the day she was caned for being late for school. 'We always got to school very early. That morning I was playing with my friend in the yard until it was time to go in. Suddenly we heard them singing hymns in assembly!' Mum's face reflected the horror she still experienced as she remembered that moment. 'We ran in as fast as we could, but we were in trouble for being late and got the cane – on both hands!' The injustice of it still smarts – as did her poor little hands.

She remembered another, happier day, her birthday, when one of the boys gave her a wonderful present – a slate! Sadly she was made to give it back. Small girls were not allowed to accept gifts from boys – even at the age of eight. They say, 'Like Mother, like daughter!' I, too, was made to return a gift from a boy-friend when I was young.

I was a 'Mixed Infant' at the time. In my class was our butcher's son, Jackie, who was rather sweet on me. One day, I remember it well, he gave me a roughly folded piece of paper bearing a transfer of a ship. When I opened it, there was a real diamond ring! I ran home in delight to show it to my mother – only to be made to give it back to Jackie's father. It had belonged to his late wife, and Jackie had found it in a drawer. So I do know how disappointed Mum must have felt when she had to return her slate to her young admirer.

We had tea with Mary and her husband, Ted, and continued to talk. Mary told us that, when she received my letter, my surname rang a bell. When she was young and living in York, her brother used to go around with a group of young fellows from Rougier Street, which included a Bill Batchelor. That was my father!

Then, blow me, another coincidence. Mary's daughter works in a Home for the disabled at New Earswick, York. One of the residents is John Batchelor, my lovely, talented cousin John! In spite of being born with cerebral palsy, almost sixty years ago, he is an active sportsman and has countless awards and medals, especially for swimming. What a small world it is, to be sure. Our visit to Easingwold was a lovely, warm experience. It never ceases to amaze me how kind total strangers can be. Family History certainly restores your faith in human nature!

Now I set myself the task of locating the house which used to be the Godfrey Walker Home, if it still existed. It was not an easy task – but then, who wants it to be easy? There would be no fun in finding all the lost pieces of a genealogical puzzle at the push of a button. It is the searching, the struggling, the frustrations and the dead ends which make it all the more wonderful when the lost information is suddenly discovered.

The Home's address was given, in Frances's case-file, as 4, West Bank Terrace, but there is no such place in York now. On an old street map I found West Bank Nurseries, but that was not much help. I decided that I would have to send a few more 'grovelling

Frances with Ted and Mary Willis.
'School friends re-united' – Easingwold 1996.

letters' to solve the mystery. So I wrote to the librarian at York Reference Library – 'Dear Sir or Madam, I know you must be awfully busy, but . . .'

A gentleman from one of my Family History classes at the Swarthmore Centre, who is a great admirer of the effectiveness of my famous 'grovelling letters', once wrote to *me* , 'Dear Anne, I know *you* must be awfully busy, but . . .' It did make me chuckle.

My letter reached the Acting Local Studies Librarian, the kind and helpful Geoffrey Bowling. He wrote me several letters as he searched for the Godfrey Walker Home for me. Their tone was always apologetic, 'I'm afraid I have found very little information –'; 'I have not found West Bank Terrace on any map of the 1920s/1930s'; 'I regret that the only photographs I can find of Acomb Road show an undeveloped country lane –'; but what the wonderful man did send me, without realising it, were enough bits of the jigsaw for me to solve my problem.

He assumed that 'West Bank Terrace was the name given to the line of buildings on the right-hand side of Acomb Road, opposite West Bank Nurseries.' He sent me a copy of an Ordnance Survey map of 1929 showing such a terrace of four houses. Then, in a moment of inspiration, he photocopied for me pages from the York directories for 1920/22/27/35. It was the very last one which was to pinpoint the Home for me.

Mum had told me that – 'Doctor Hood lived in a big house in its own grounds, next door to the Home.' The 1935 directory lists – 'Hood, Dr. Noel, Howe Hill,' followed by – 'Godfrey Walker Home, 4 West Bank Terrace'! Clever old Mum! Two houses away on the list was our old friend – 'Birks, Edmund Alfred,' the Colonel at West Garth.

What was so wonderful about the 1935 directory was that, unlike the previous ones which listed the streets alphabetically, this one listed them *as walked*. That is, it gives the inhabitants of Moorgate and Hobgate, streets on the left hand side of Acomb Road which still exist today and therefore whose location can be confirmed, and follows that with the wonderfully significant note, 'Return, right-hand side,' (i.e. across the road, opposite Moorgate and Hobgate) 'West Garth – Howe Hill – Godfrey Walker Home.'

I decided to write to Mrs. Freedman, the York City Archivist, who had been so helpful to me many years ago when I was a raw and ignorant beginner in Family History. I thought that she might have some records or photographs of the elusive Home. Sadly she had nothing, but yet again a casual note at the end of her letter helped me pinpoint the very house which had been Godfrey Walker.

'The building is still in existence,' she wrote, 'if you want to look at it for yourself. Apparently the number has now changed. We think it would now be 134, Acomb Road.' Bless the lady! I would never have guessed that 4, West Bank Terrace was masquerading under the new address of 134, Acomb Road!

I now wrote a letter to 'The Occupier, 134, Acomb Road,' explaining my quest and asking whether they would mind if I brought Mum to look at the house and took photographs. The reply came from the owner of 134, explaining that it is now converted into private flats. Her husband confirmed that it was once a Children's Home.

She had no objections to our visit and photographs, but she explained that it would only be possible for me to take Mum into the entrance hall and not into any of the rooms. I quite understood, and wrote a letter to the occupier of the ground-floor flat, telling them that I would be bringing Mum on Mother's Day. I did not want them to come across us in the vestibule and think we were geriatric burglars!

So it was that on Mother's Day, 1996, Frances Batchelor, née Harrap, once again crossed the threshold of the Godfrey Walker Home. She had entered that door as a motherless child of six and passed out through the same door as a fifteen-year-old to face the world alone. Both must have been terrifying moments for her.

She had only been back through that door on one other occasion, in 1938, when she returned to show off her new-born baby – me! – to the Matron and girls. I think that signifies just what the Home meant to her. The people there were her family. The Matron and Sister had been invited to her wedding at St. Paul's Church in 1936, and it was to them she returned with her child, to share her joy with them.

Now, in her old age, she had crossed the threshold yet again, with her grown-up daughter. It was a very moving moment which I shall never forget. Frances had come home.

CHAPTER THREE

MABEL'S LOST MADONNA

Captain Locker of the 13/18th Hussars, in the foreword to my book about *My Gallant Hussar*, described me thus – 'Like a dog with a bone, she will not let go and is quite ingenious in her methods of finding new tracks down which to patrol. She is the most enthusiastic sifter and delver of records that I have ever had the pleasure to meet!' I think the story of my search for Mabel's Madonna justifies that compliment.

From the York directories sent to me by my friends at York City Library I was able to list some of the Matrons who had mothered my little Frances during her ten years at Godfrey Walker.

1920 – GERTRUDE AND SARAH PRICE
1922 – ALICE LOUISA PEARSON
1927 to 1934 – MABEL WOOD

Mabel Wood is the one my mother remembers best. She was Matron for her last three years in the Home, in those very important years of her life between twelve and fifteen, and was extremely kind to her.

It was Miss Wood who helped Frances keep in touch with her little brother, Will, when he was in the Bede Home for Waifs and Strays at Wakefield. She took Frances to Wakefield to visit him at his school, where the class sang some songs for their little visitor. Then Miss Wood took the two children out to tea in a café. What an exciting experience for them. It was a birthday treat for Frances, who remembers having cakes and a glass of milk.

When they took Will back to the Bede Home at the end of the visit, Miss Wood mentioned that it was Frances' birthday. A few days later a parcel arrived in the post. The staff at Will's Home had sent her a dress for her birthday. Not a 'hand-me-down' from one of the older Godfrey Walker girls, as she usually wore, but a new dress of her very own, in pale buttercup yellow. With it was a matching straw hat with flowers round the brim. With her thick golden hair, she must have looked like a little princess.

Mabel Wood was Matron when Frances left in 1929 to go into service, but they kept in touch and she sent her 'old girl' a studio photograph of herself as a keepsake. It had been taken by the same Coney Street photographer who, in 1923, had taken a lovely picture of Frances as a sweet-faced child of ten. Mum has no idea why it was taken. Perhaps it was for her father? She remembers that a huge copy of it hung in the photographer's window for weeks. That must have made her feel very special, bless her.

The Godfrey Walker Matron in 1936, when my parents married, was a

Original photograph of Mabel's Madonna

Miss Forsythe, and the Sister was Mrs. Barnes. Mrs. Barnes came to the wedding and afterwards told Frances the sad news that Miss Wood had died. 'I know that you were very fond of her,' she said, 'Perhaps you would like this photograph. It shows a memorial to her, in the Lady Chapel of her church.' She gave Frances a tiny photograph of a Madonna and Child which she has treasured for over sixty years in her box of special family photographs.

Looking at it one day I asked her, 'Would you like me to find out where it is? Then we could take some flowers in gratitude for her kindness.' Mum thought that was a lovely idea. I was not to know what a long and convoluted search it was going to be. It was to be over a year before I stood in front of Mabel's Madonna and placed our flowers there.

It all sounded so simple. Twice every Sunday Mabel had taken the Godfrey Walker girls to church at St. Paul's, Holgate Road. Naturally, that was where the Madonna would be – or so I thought. A letter explaining my quest went off to the Vicar of St. Paul's, along with a copy of the photograph. Although time had faded the tiny picture, it clearly showed a full length figure with a child in her arms. She stood on a shelf which bore a small brass plaque. There were flowers in a vase below, a brick wall behind and three stone steps leading into the Lady Chapel, which had a stained-glass window.

I sat back happily to await confirmation that it was at St. Paul's – and was stunned to receive a letter from the Vicar, telling me that he had no knowledge of it ever having been there. Perhaps it might be in Acomb Church? But no, there was no sign of it there. Now the hunt was up!

I wrote dozens of letters to York churches; to Mrs. Freedman at the City Archives; to the *Yorkshire Evening Post* and *Evening Press*; to the Yorkshire Archaeological Society; to the *Dalesman* Magazine; to Mr. Bowling at the Local Studies Library – every letter containing a copy of my tiny photograph, with the request that it be pinned up on their notice board.

Soon I had my spies out all over York. One elderly gentleman, Frank Atkinson, thought he saw it on an old photograph of St. Sampson's Church in 1929, but it wasn't my statue. Pity! Then another gentleman, George Robson, thought he recognised it in the park where he went bowling – which was quite close to the Godfrey Walker Home. Sadly, the Parks Department told me that it was, in fact, '– the statue of an elderly gentleman.' Foiled again!

A number of my spies turned up at St. Paul's Church, convinced that it must have been there, to the great frustration of the vicar. When I visited the wonderful York Family History Fair, at the Racecourse, I wore a copy of the photograph pinned to my blouse, with the word, 'HELP!' written across it in large letters. Still no joy. I did wonder whether some low-church vicar had decided that he did not want such high-church images in his church. Perhaps Mabel's Madonna had been banished to the cellar, waiting sixty long years for me to come and rescue her.

I discovered that, when such a memorial was erected, a 'faculty' giving official permission had to be obtained. I wrote to the Borthwick Institute at York, who confirmed this, but they pointed out that to find the faculty for Mabel's Madonna it was necessary to know the name of the church! Back to square one.

I even wrote, in desperation, to the Archivist at Bishopthorpe Palace, the home of the Archbishop of York. When in doubt, go right to the top. That's my philosophy! Their librarian was not able to help either, but the photograph was sent to the Rural Dean, who passed it round at meetings. Still no luck. Mabel's Madonna had vanished.

There was nothing for it but to do some research on Mabel Wood herself. I noticed that some previous Matrons appeared on group photographs in the habit of Anglican nuns. The librarian at Bishopthorpe Palace was able to tell me that the mother-house of their order was the Convent of the Holy Paraclete at Whitby. Perhaps, I thought, our Madonna was in the convent chapel? Another letter, another copy of the photograph – another negative reply.

If I could discover where Mabel died, that would narrow down my search. I had no idea of the date but the personal photograph she had given my mother was dated on the back by the York photographer at his Coney Street studio as 1931. Such dating should be compulsory! It would be such a help to family historians who inherit wonderful photographs of stern-faced ladies in tight stays and jet jewellery, with no chance of discovering who they are.

I knew that Mabel was no longer alive when my parents married in 1936, the date the tiny photograph was given to my mother. It would therefore be easy to find her death, I thought, for it was clearly between 1931 and 1936. I went merrily down to the claustrophobic St. Cath's Room at the Leeds Reference Library, where there is an index of countrywide births, marriages and deaths, from 1837, on microfilm. It shouldn't be difficult to find Mabel, I thought. It was just a matter of trawling through the Wood deaths. Then I would go and do some shopping. I should have known better!

I started twirling the handle of my microfilm reader, gently cursing her for having a surname right at the end of the alphabet. Searching for Batchelors is so much easier. There should be a Government Health Warning printed on microfilm readers. Using one for hour after hour does awful things to the tendons of the wrist, and results in strangely blurred vision on stepping out into daylight at the end of a session. If/when I win the lottery, I shall throw out all the old, stiff readers and replace them with eight electrically operated models which are sheer bliss to use. Until that day, I will just settle for getting locked in one night with a tin of WD40!

As I twirled away, aiming for the Wood entries at the far end of the microfilm for 1931, I glanced around at the other researchers at nearby readers. I remembered, with a smile, the comment of my *Timewatch* producer, Antonia, when we were filming my adventures for BBC2 eight years ago. 'Good heavens,' she said. 'They look like a shed-full of battery hens!' From the glazed expressions on their faces, I could easily work out who had been there since opening-time.

I began to wonder what they thought about while twirling. Did they, like me, hallucinate and talk to their quarry? 'Come on, Mabel. Stop playing hard-to-get! I know you're there somewhere.' Perhaps they were planning their next grovelling letter – 'Dear Sir/Madam, I know you must be awfully busy, but HELP! My grandfather was married and died, but doesn't appear to have ever been born!'

Maybe they were thinking up an excuse for their spouse waiting at home – 'I *know* I said that I would only spend an hour at the library, dear, but I felt in my bones that today I would find Great-grandma, so I just had to keep going! Besides, my watch stopped.' A likely story! The truth of the matter is that family research is addictive. It is impossible to stop twirling unless the eyes mist over, or a member of staff enters the room shaking a bunch of keys and shouts, 'Closing in five minutes!' It is very noticeable how, as closing-time approaches, the winding of film becomes more frantic and the tables rock and roll in an alarming manner.

So I twirled my handle and muttered to Mabel Wood under my breath. Occasionally there would be a cry of delight/disbelief/relief as some poor soul *at last* found their Gertrude Matilda. I was amazed at the number of Mabel Woods who died between 1931 and 1936. There were fifteen of them. That did not include the 'Mabel Louise's, the 'Mabel Sophie's or the 'Mabel Dora's – Not forgetting all the *Woods* ladies.

Some of the fifteen could be ruled out because they would be the wrong age to fit the photograph we had of our Mabel in 1931. I guessed her age to be late forties or perhaps early fifties. That left me with eleven Mabel Woods, dying all over the country from Middlesbrough to Brighton, and as far away from York as Bideford in Devon. If she were not among these eleven then she had a second Christian name, and there were a further *nineteen* of them!

It was time now for me to start sending my 'boomerang cheques'. To obtain a death certificate I made out a cheque for £5.50, payable to 'The Superintendent Registrar', and sent it with a letter to the first Register Office on my list, asking for the death certificate of their Mabel Wood – 'But only if she is given as single. Her occupation would probably be something to do with children or another of the caring professions. If your Mabel does not fit this description please return my cheque.' Like a homing-pigeon, back it came, minus a certificate.

Gradually I worked my way down my list of Mabels. Like clockwork my cheque was returned to me by the registrars, with the depressing news, 'Sorry. the details are not as you have given,' or more helpfully, 'Sorry! Our Mabel Wood was a widow.' The same cheque travelled the length and breadth of the land, dropping into the post-box and back through my letter-box with monotonous regularity. Eventually I would have to replace it, as it became too obviously out-of-date, making out a new boomerang cheque to succeed it, and waiting gloomily for it to wend its way home again.

I started with the register offices nearest to York, hoping that Mabel had been a Yorkshire lass. Gradually the circle widened and I was finally left with just three possibilities. They were Brighton, Bideford and Pancras (London). I wanted, in my heart of hearts, not to find her in London, which is a deadly difficult area to research. So I chose Brighton.

Simon, my postie.

Mabel Wood

Some days later I had a phone call from a most helpful registrar called Rosina. She wanted to read the details of her Mabel Wood to me over the phone, '– because I don't want you to waste your money on the wrong certificate'. Bless the lady! How kind! Her Mabel was single, but a seamstress, with a father who was a platelayer on the railway. Although it was possible that my Mabel could have earned her living doing sewing, it was not what I had expected, and the Brighton Mabel was rather young for our 1931 photograph. Their lady would have been thirty-seven when she became Matron and only just forty-one in our photograph.

Possible, I suppose, but not probable. 'Anyway,' said Rosina, 'Keep our Mabel in mind and if you can't find her anywhere else, come back to us.' Such kindness.

That left me with just two other Mabels, one in Devon and the other in London. I found it hard to believe that a woman from Devon would find her way to a post in Yorkshire, so with a heavy sigh I turned my attention to the Mabel Wood whose death was registered at Pancras. When my young postie, Simon, brought me my self-addressed envelope, I could feel that it contained a certificate. Had I found our Mabel at last? My fingers trembled with anticipation as I tore open the long brown envelope.

The enclosed certificate was for a Mabel Wood who died at University College Hospital on 5 November, 1935. She was fifty-nine, and had lived at 31, Leamington Road Villas, Paddington, with her sister, R. S. Wood. Her occupation? 'A Retired Matron, Children's Home.' 'Oh, Mabel!' I said out loud, and with great emotion, 'God love you, Mabel! Gotcha!'

The certificate contained a wealth of information. Besides showing that she lived with her unmarried sister R.S., who was the informant, it gave more family details at the foot of the 'Occupation' column. She was, it said, 'Daughter of Charles Wood, a master grocer (deceased).'

Now it would be easy to find the lost Madonna. She would be in the nearest church to Leamington Road Villas. A piece of cake! I wrote a grovelling letter to the nearest public library, addressing it to – 'Paddington Public Library, London.' I enclosed a copy of the tiny photograph, asking for it to be pinned to the library notice board, and entrusted my envelope to my wonderful friends at the Royal Mail.

Good for them! It reached the librarian, who sent me a copy of a page from the London AtoZ, showing the exact location of Leamington Road Villas. There were a number of churches nearby, each signified by a small cross, but – frustration! – with no names marked. There was even one slap on the end of Leamington Road Villas. I felt I was nearing the end of my quest.

The librarian, showing the kind helpfulness which never ceases to amaze me, then forwarded my letter to Susannah Rayner, the senior archivist at the City of Westminster Archive Centre. She sent me pages from the London Diocese Book for 1996 and suggested that St. Stephen's was probably the nearest church still in use. She, in turn, passed my letter to Tom Gillum at St. Stephen's. He told me that St. Stephen's had been closed and neglected until 1994, when it re-opened. Sadly, he didn't recognise our Madonna, nor its setting beside the three Lady Chapel steps.

I still had a feeling in my bones about the church marked on the map at the end of Mabel's road. Studying the pages from the Diocese Book again, I surmised that it was probably St. Luke's, closed in 1947. I bet my boots that our Madonna had been there. It was the obvious church for Mabel and her sister to attend. As the church had been closed, presumably the memorial had gone elsewhere – but where? Certainly not to St. Stephen's

Perhaps I was fooling myself and I would never find it. Perhaps my first idea was correct, that it had been in a church bombed in the 1940s, or consigned to a dark cellar by a low-church vicar. Perhaps I was indeed flogging a dead horse. My problem is that I am a profound optimist and I just could not believe that I would never find it. So I pressed on.

As I had the exact date of Mabel's death, I thought I would look for her will. Surely a well-educated and efficient woman such as she undoubtedly was would have left a will. No, she didn't! As she died of pneumonia, hemiplegia of the right side and cerebral tumour, poor lady, she obviously had something like a stroke and was not able to put her affairs in order before she died.

Instead of a will I found a grant of letters of administration to another sister, Kate Letitia Wood, who also lived at 31, Leamington Road Villas. Mabel was described as 'a spinster without parent' and Kate Letitia as 'lawful sister of the whole blood and one of the persons entitled to share in the estate of the said intestate'. Mabel left £861 7s. 10d.

She had died at the University College Hospital, so perhaps her Madonna was in the hospital chapel? The chaplain was apologetic but 'I have checked the service register of the time and there is no mention of the dedication of a memorial gift in the appropriate period.' Foiled again!

A friend of mine suggested that the statue looked decidedly Roman Catholic. Could Mabel have converted in the last years of her life? I wrote to Westminster R.C. Cathedral in London, but they could not help. I tried Lambeth Palace, too, but no joy there either. I was beginning to feel desperate – but I just couldn't admit defeat.

Perhaps I was concentrating too much on Mabel's death. Maybe it would help if I discovered her birthplace instead. Could it be that her Madonna had been given to the family church where she had been christened and confirmed? As I expected that there would be dozens of Mabel Woods in the St. Catherine's Index of Births, I decided to take a short cut and look for her on census returns instead.

Unfortunately there is a hundred-year secrecy rule covering census information, so I would not be able to pick her up on the York census of 1931. Instead, I would have to use either the 1881 or 1891 census returns for London. In 1881 she would only be a tiny child, if my estimation of her age from the Coney Street photograph was correct, so she might just be there.

The advantage of using the '81 rather than the '91 is that it has been indexed by county and by personal name. The Mormon Church – better known as the Church of Jesus Christ of Latter Day Saints – together with family historians all over the country, completed this monumental task last year. The resulting index is a brilliant finding-aid.

I visited my local Mormon Church's Family History Library, where their facilities are most generously made available, free of charge, to non-members of their church such as me. There I saw the 1881 index for Middlesex, which includes London. Frustration! There was no little Mabel Wood. There *was* a Charles Wood, grocer, living in Islington with a small family, but he had no Kate Letitia or R.S. among his children. Was that Mabel's grocer father? I had my doubts. Then it dawned on me – 'London' covers not only Middlesex but also Surrey.

There, on the Surrey census for 1881, was a little Mabel Wood aged four, with a father Charles Wood, a grocer, and a baby sister Kate Letitia. Wonderful stuff! They lived in Camberwell, and Mabel's birthplace was given as Dulwich. Now I had two more areas to search for our Madonna.

I sent a cluster of grovelling letters to all the churches in Camberwell and Dulwich, each containing a copy of our tiny photograph. I wrote to the local libraries, asking for the photograph and accompanying cry for help to be pinned up on their notice board. It is what I believe is called 'saturation bombing'. I send lots of letters at once, in the firm belief that one will hit the target. It takes too long to await individual replies in turn. The result of all these letters? Not a sausage!

It must be obvious to my readers that I qualify for the Customer of the Year award from the Post Office. I imagine I could paper the walls of my flat with the number of postage stamps I buy in a year. When I visit my local Post Office each Monday, I smile to myself as the man in front asks for, 'Two second class stamps and one first, please.' Then it is my turn. 'Thirty second class and ten first, please.' That just about lasts me a week. My nice young postie will never be made redundant while I am busy with family history research! I remember once being out with Mum when we saw a massive red pantechnicon bearing the words, 'ROYAL MAIL'. 'Ah,' said Mum, 'I see your post is arriving.'

I tried the churches of Stepney, where Mabel's father was born and her parents were married. Nothing. I was getting desperate. I tried all the tricks in the book – and a few of my own. I began writing to other people who were researching the name Wood. I advertised in the wonderful *Family Tree Magazine.*

I advertised my quest on Teletext's *Lost Touch* service, hoping to find a descendant of Charles Wood's family. All I got were two letters. One was from a helpful lady, Shirley Hedger, who used to have a cab office near Leamington Road Villas and whose friend actually lived in the basement flat at No. 31, Mabel's home.

The other letter, from Brenda Gorman née Wood, told me that her family were from the Dulwich area, where our Mabel was born, and that her father had a brother called Charles. There was, however, no obvious link with Mabel's family. I had every sympathy with an aptly named gentleman who ended his Teletext advertisement with the words, 'If you can help, please ring me *Ivor Hunt on* 0181 123 4567.' You and me both, mate!

I thought that I was at last back on the trail of the lost Madonna when I received a letter from Rev. Powell of Christ Church and Upton Chapel, in London. He told me that there was a church in South Lambeth Road, called St. Anne's and All Saints, which, according to the plaque outside it, was associated with the Waifs and Strays Society. Apparently it was Edward Rudolf's church. Eager for a result after all these months of dead ends, I wrote to the vicar. He denied all knowledge of our Madonna. Do you wonder my hair has turned white? It's a wonder I haven't torn it out in frustration!

I have to admit I was running out of ideas. I felt now that all I could do was to sit back and wait. I must have sent dozens of letters and copies of our photograph all over the country. Surely someone out there would recognise Mabel's Madonna?

One morning, just over a year since I made that rash promise to my mother that I would find the memorial for her, my postie Simon handed me my usual heap of junk mail and unwanted catalogues. Sandwiched in the middle was a long white envelope postmarked 'London'. I opened it quite casually, and saw that it was from another London church – one that I had not written to. The letter heading showed a sketch of All Saints, Notting Hill, and the writer was Rev. Prebendary John Brownsell.

He wrote -

> 'Dear Miss Batchelor,
> Your statue now resides in my church, having come from St. Stephen's, Paddington, where it was taken after the war from its original home in St. Luke's.'

How can I describe how I felt? Incredulous – elated – hysterical almost! It was a combination of winning the lottery and reaching the summit of Everest! So my instinct had been right. Mabel's Madonna had originally been placed in the church at the end of her street. At once I was on the phone to Rev. Brownsell, to thank him in person. All I got was an answering machine telling me that he was not available. I tried the next day and got the same blessed machine. The message ended, 'However, if you urgently need to speak to a priest, ring this number –'. I rang it, and got a poor lady out of her bath.

She was the wife of Father Duguid (what a lovely name for a priest!) and she told me to ring again that evening. I waited impatiently for the evening and then spoke with Father Duguid. He told me that Father Brownsell had gone to America but he would be back in a few weeks.

Meanwhile he gave me details of the church and confirmed that there was indeed a Madonna and Child, but with no plaque to identify it as Mabel's. He invited me to visit the church sometime and share in the Morning Mass which was celebrated at 11 am. As soon as I got some free time in my busy life I planned a visit. Sadly, Mum would not be able to go with me, for the long journey to London would be too much for her, but I could represent her and take our flowers in memory of kind Mabel Wood.

When Father Brownsell eventually came back from his travel, I spoke to him and arranged my visit. I was a little

31, Leamington Road Villas, where Mabel lived with her sisters.

apprehensive about walking through Notting Hill on my own. After all, there are some parts of my own home town of Leeds that I would not walk around on my own, even in daylight. Father Brownsell said that some visitors did feel a little uneasy about Notting Hill, so he suggested that I use a taxi from the Tube station.

So it was that I found myself hurtling towards All Saints in one of London's famous black cabs, clutching a bunch of beautiful spring flowers to place on Mabel's memorial. As usual, the driver chatted to me and asked where I was from. Obviously my Yorkshire accent marked me, in his book, as a foreigner. I explained my mission and asked whether we could take a detour to see Leamington Road Villas on the way to the church.

Of course, he had never heard of them, so together we pored over my photocopied page from an old street map. Eventually we found the street, and coasted along looking for number 31. I'll bet all the local Neighbourhood Watch were sitting up and taking notice behind their lace curtains!

At last, there it was. I found it quite eerie to reach the house where Mabel had spent her last months with her sisters, Kate Letitia and 'R. S.' I suppose she must have been completely dependent on them. I was glad that she who had spent her days caring for the girls at the Godfrey Walker Home at York was, in her turn, cared for by her family.

I leapt out of my cab to take a photograph of the rather fine house at number 31. I had imagined that the area would be seedy and run-down, but instead the houses were neat and well cared-for. Then, to escape the clutches of the Neighbourhood Watch, I dashed back to my taxi and full speed ahead to All Saints, passing the site of St. Luke's at the end of Mabel's street. How I wished I could have found the Madonna there, where it had been placed by her grieving family in 1935.

Heart beating rapidly with excitement and anticipation, I arrived at the entrance to All Saints Church, to find that I was half an hour early for the 11 a.m. Mass. I have always had this terrible fear of being late, so I always over-estimate how long a journey will take me. Whenever I take a taxi from home to Leeds City Station I always arrive with about forty minutes to spare, and have to mooch about the bookshop to kill time. Still, it's better than dashing in at the last minute. It's against my religion to rush!

The church was already open so I wandered in, past a stunning, almost life-size crucifix set against a blood red curtain. At first glance there was no sign of Mabel's Madonna. I really had no idea how large she was going to be. It was difficult to estimate size from our tiny faded photograph. I walked slowly down the side aisle and came upon a pair of wrought-iron gates in the side wall. I stopped dead in my tracks. There she was!

In a side corridor, next to a plain glass window, on a small wooden table stood Mabel's Madonna. She was *beautiful*. The figure was far larger than I had imagined, about two-thirds life-size, the paintwork fresh and bright. She gathered her blue cloak with her right hand – I recognised every fold of that cloak from our photograph. She looked down at the tiny, sleeping Child nestled in the crook of her neck, and her head was inclined towards Him so that His curls brushed her cheek. Her face was serenely beautiful. I was stunned.

After all those months that I had been searching, twelve in all, I was not prepared for the intense emotion which swept over me. I was so glad that the church was still empty, so that I could have those few moments alone to compose myself. The whole feeling conveyed by the Madonna was of such great tenderness and love. It was, I felt, a fitting memorial to Mabel Wood, who had been so kind to my little mother and the other girls in her care at York.

With a deep sense of gratitude I placed my bunch of spring flowers beside the Madonna. With it was a small card on which I had written:

> 'In loving memory of dear Mabel Wood, Matron of the Godfrey Walker Waifs and Strays Home, York, in gratitude for her kindness. From one of her little girls, Frances Batchelor née Harrap, aged 83.'

I was now joined by a jolly West Indian lady who welcomed me to the church and introduced herself as Adelaide. I explained who I was and why I had brought flowers to Mabel's Madonna. She offered to take a couple of photographs for me, to capture the moment for my

All Saints, Notting Hill

At last – the lost Madonna!

mother. When they were later developed I found that on the first one she had cut off the Madonna's head and the other cut me in half! However, by cleverly combining the two photographs I now have a wonderful record of my moment of joy.

Then Father Brownsell arrived to conduct the Mass for Ash Wednesday. Adelaide, bless her, decided to adopt this visitor from the wilds of Yorkshire. 'You sit with me,' she said, so I joined the tiny congregation consisting of an elderly nun in a grey habit, seven West Indian ladies, Adelaide and me. The service was simple and very moving. The congregation knew the responses by heart so there was no service book. Instead Adelaide would hiss, 'Now we stand!' and 'Sit!' in my ear.

After the service I had a long talk with Father Brownsell, a kindly and gentle man, who showed great interest in the story of his Madonna. He told me that when St. Luke's, her original home at the end of Mabel's street, was closed, she was passed to St. Stephen's. When St. Stephen's closed she moved again, to All Saints where no-one knew that she was a personal memorial.

So how did Father Brownsell come to write to me, out of the blue? Apparently two old parishioners who used to worship at St. Luke's many years ago saw my photograph of the Madonna – either in their local library or local newspaper, Father Brownsell was not sure. I *knew* that if I saturated London with our photograph, someone somewhere would recognise it eventually. This couple then approached Father Brownsell and said, 'Isn't that *our* Madonna?'

Bless them. If they had not recognised it, I might never have had the moving experience of laying our floral tribute before her, in grateful memory of dear, kind Matron Mabel Wood.

CHAPTER FOUR

THIS LITTLE CHAP

It must have been a heart-wrenching sight, in the spring of 1920, when six-year-old Frances parted company with her little brother, Will. She was off to a new life in the Godfrey Walker Home at York. But what of Will? What became of him?

All that she remembers is that in her later years at Godfrey Walker, her brother was in a Home at Wakefield and that when he was older, he joined the Royal Fusiliers as a boy-soldier and bandsman. She remembers the awful day in 1944 when she received news of his death in Italy.

I remember that day, too. I was six-years-old. I came running in from school at dinner-time, and found no dinner awaiting me. Instead, Mum sat at the table, crying and clutching a telegram. I begged her to tell me what was wrong. 'You won't understand,' she said through her tears. 'I will – tell me,' I insisted. She told me that my Uncle Bill had died in the war and would never be coming home again. Even at that tender age I recognised the enormity of this news, and to this day I remember every word of that conversation.

I have only two memories of my soldier-uncle. I remember him visiting our home at Seacroft with his young wife, Molly, and coming to meet me from school. Hand in hand the three of us ran laughing down the steep road, and several times they lifted their arms so that I flew through the air.

My other memory is of being lifted up by him so that I could touch the kitchen ceiling. I felt so clever! These two small cameos are all I remember of him, but I was aware, even at that early age, of the strong bond between him and my mother. This bond was all the more amazing because they had been parted for so many of their growing-up years.

As the Children's Society had managed to locate Mum's personal case-file, containing so much detail of her childhood, I wondered whether they might also have her brother's. I expected that they would be little more than duplicates of hers. I couldn't have been more wrong. It took their wonderful Archivist, Ian, and his assistant, Dawn, months and months to locate the file from over seventy years ago. Thankfully they never gave up the search, in spite of being kept extremely busy tracing records of more recent children.

'This little chap' – Will aged about 14.

So one wonderful morning my postie, Simon, handed me a large, heavy brown envelope, stamped with the Children's Society logo. It contained even more documents than those in Mum's file – over seventy in all. There were many letters, including one in the familiar hand of dear Sister Tomlinson at the Pontefract Mother and Baby Home. She describes again the reason for the two children needing a home, and gives a thumbnail sketch of my little mother which I had not seen before:

> 'She seems a nice child. She came to us last Saturday and is quite contented and very obedient.'

The file contained numerous letters from her over the next two months, as she pestered the Waifs and Strays Society to take these two motherless children off her hands. She says of their father, 'I really think that he would like them brought up in a Home for their spiritual and temporal training. He seems anxious about them.'

Once again the documents show my poor grandfather signing away all rights to his child, knowing that this was the best he could do for little Will. So four-year-old William Samuel Harrap was packed off to the Society's Receiving House in Clapham Road, London, to be 'sorted out'. He sounds like a little lost parcel. He was only there for two weeks, then he was sent to a foster-mother in Norwich, a Miss Jane Hall who lived in the village of Frettenham.

The case-file contains a copy of her 'Form of Undertaking', in which she promises

> 'to bring up William Harrop (sic) as one of my own children, and to provide him with proper food, lodging, medical attendance and washing, and for the proper repair and renewal of clothing, and to endeavour to train him in habits of truthfulness, obedience, personal cleanliness and industry; as well as in suitable domestic and outdoor work; to provide the said child with a separate bed, to take care that the said child, William Harrop, shall attend duly at church, and shall, while boarded out between the ages of four and twelve years, attend Day and Sunday Schools, unless prevented by sickness or other urgent cause, during all the usual hours for instruction thereat.'

Miss Hall also promised that he would have a medical examination by a lady doctor twice a year. Her home is described as follows: 'Three-bedrooms, sitting room and kitchen. It is clean and comfortable.' The case-file describes William at this time as, 'Height – 3½ ft, weight 2 st. 7¾ lb, chest measurement – 20½ ins'.

I did try to find the other little boys who were with Jane Hall at the time he was there. One of the wonderful documents in his case-file gave their names as Donald Robinson and Leslie Hardy. Using Channel 4's *Lost Touch* service, I asked whether anyone knew of these two old gentlemen now in their eighties. I was hoping that someone would reply, 'Yes, that is my grandfather, and he remembers your William Harrap!' I was hoping for some memories of his lost childhood, but sadly no-one replied.

By the following February, 1921, my grandfather had decided that Norfolk was too far away for him to visit and he was anxious to keep in touch with his young son. Because this meant a great deal to him, he nattered the Society for the next couple of months, asking them to move the child to a Home in the North, where he could maintain a firm relationship with his son.

In April a place was found for William at All Saints, Almondbury, Huddersfield. There was some problem getting the little lad there, however. The local vicar describes the problem which arose when he tried to put him on the train at Norwich, in the care of the guard:

> 'In the station-master's office, I expressed my anxiety at sending so young a child on a nine-hour journey with at least two changes, and was told that by a recent rule no guard is allowed to accept the care of a child travelling alone. I was further told that, in their opinion, it was unsafe to send him.'

Perhaps they had heard about little Frances and her adventures at Pontefract Station!

Eventually little Willie Harrap arrived at Huddersfield, where he stayed for four years before being sent to the Bede Home at Wakefield, which was closer to his father's home at Featherstone. In the *Waifs and Strays Magazine* I managed to find him on two group photographs taken during his time there. Some of the boys looked poor, sad children, but he is bright-faced and smiling, just like his sister on her photographs.

Reading through the masses of letters and documents

in his case-file, I couldn't help but be impressed by the real concern shown by all the officials of the Society. It was interesting, too, to see how he was described – 'this lad –' '– this little chap –', '– this little fellow –' and '– this young boy –'. All of these, to me, suggest affectionate concern. His name, too, appears in different forms. At home he was always known to the family as 'our Will'. The Society called him, '– little Willie Harrap,' and I knew him as Uncle Bill.

The Bede Home was not too far from York, so now he was able to re-establish his relationship with his sister, Frances. They visited each other, courtesy of Matron Mabel Wood, and sent each other cards

Bede Home, Wakefield.
(Courtesy of G. Steenton).

Ian Wakeling, Archivist of the Children's Society with George Steenton, an old Bede boy.

and letters. Frances even received a card from one of his friends at the Bede Home. It was from a boy called Maurice. She had never met him, but Maurice's card bore a mass of kisses! I decided to see whether Maurice had survived to the 1990s. The Miss Marple in me loves the challenge of a mystery. Once again I advertised on *Lost Touch* – and found Maurice's daughter!

She told me that, sadly, Maurice had died, but she was able to tell me something about him. He had been born in 1916, making him just a year younger that Will. He had been adopted by a couple called Cawthorne from Barnsley. She gave a beautiful and loving description of him. She wrote, 'All his life he was a good husband and father, and the finest gentleman who ever lived.' What a lovely tribute. I wish I could have found him in time for us to meet.

Will Harrap spent five years in the Bede Home, where he proved very useful in the garden. Then I read, with mounting surprise, that it had been decided to send him to Canada on the Child Migrant Scheme. My blood ran cold as I read document after document, listing the sailing dates and name of the ship – *S.S. Doric*, sailing from Liverpool.

I had only recently read the awful story of the Child Migrant Scheme in Margaret Humphrey's moving book, *Empty Cradles*. Although some of the children sent to Australia and Canada by the churches and the children's charities lived happy and successful lives, far too many of the poor little souls lived in misery – at best as slaves and skivvies, and in many cases abused, both physically and sexually. The only childhood photograph Mum had of him shows a sweet-faced , fair-haired boy. I shuddered to think what his fate might have been.

When I mentioned Canada to Mum, she told me that she remembers Will being brought to York by 'two men in suits'. He had come to say goodbye to his sister. It must have been a poignant moment. This brother and sister who had been so close for the first four years of their lives, who had been parted for five years and then re-united when Will came to a Home in Yorkshire, were now saying what could be their last goodbyes. I'll bet there were some tears. Even the gentlemen in suits must have been touched.

However, he never went. I breathed a sigh of relief. The

Young Will Harrap.

Canadian Emigration Department decided, in its wisdom, that Will Harrap had 'poor physique', he was underweight and 'small in stature'. Thank heavens for that! The Waifs and Strays Society felt that he might be very disappointed at the decision, so they moved him again, with his father's permission, to Standon Farm Home in Staffordshire, where they hoped that he would fatten up and re-apply to Canada in a few years time. It must have been a difficult decision for my grandfather to make, after all his efforts to keep in touch with his son. He must have felt that Will had a better chance of a good life in Canada, so he put his son's happiness before his own feelings. What a good father.

By this time Will was approaching sixteen and disappointed at his rejection by the Canadian authorities. He decided to make his own decisions about his future. So on 12 May, 1931, he was discharged from the care of the Society and enlisted, at Stoke-on-Trent, with the Royal Fusiliers as a boy-soldier and bandsman. It was not an unusual move. Girls from charity homes usually went into service, where their employer provided them with a home, food and clothing. Boys would gravitate towards the army, which became their family and provided for all their physical needs.

When Will first joined the Fusiliers, Frances lost track of him, for he was sent all over the country and she was in service, moving from household to household around the York area. When she became concerned that they had lost touch, she asked the Salvation Army to help her find him. Happily they were able to reunite the brother and sister. When Will had his leave, he spent it with Frances and her husband in Leeds. They were his only family, for my grandfather had died at an early age. Then, when Will married Molly White, an eighteen-year-old land-girl from Hampshire, they spent their honeymoon with Frances and Bill. This was the visit I remembered in 1943, when I was not quite six.

At the back of her dressing-table drawer, Mum keeps two bundles of yellowing letters. One contains Dad's letters to her, written during their whirlwind courtship. The other is a collection of airmail letters from her brother, Will, written during his last few months with the Royal Fusiliers in Italy in 1944.

For me, researching the story of his life, they reveal the man I hardly knew. They show, too, the close bond which still existed between brother and sister. When I carefully unwrapped the bundle of his letters from Italy, I found that they covered the last three months of his life. He wrote one to Frances every week, without fail. It was very moving to read them, for here were the thoughts and words which revealed to me a real person, rather than just a name. Not only that but they gave a very personal view of the war in Italy.

He wrote:

> 'A world of good plums and peaches are now coming into season and the grapes are beginning to take shape. On my travels I have seen what is left of the town of Cassino. I have had my baptism of fire and don't feel too grand about it, but don't worry about me, dear. I will look after myself. We get a very hearty welcome in every village we go through, and plenty of wine offered us, but we haven't time to stop for that!'

He advised Frances:

> 'Whatever you do after this war is over, dear, don't come to this "dump" after a pleasant holiday. You will go mad with all the flies there are. It must be here the world's supplies of them are bred.'

The flies, of course, were attracted by all the dead soldiers and the carnage of war. Sadly, in spite of his warning, Mum did visit Italy just once – to visit his grave.

It appears that I wrote him a letter, too, when I was only six, for in one of his letters to his sister, he wrote:

> 'Anne is getting very good at writing. No wonder you are proud of her, dear. It was very nice of her to write and she certainly writes very well.'

Little did he know that one day I would be writing his story. It brought tears to my eyes when, at the end of one letter, he sent '– kisses for Anne from Uncle Bill,' followed by three rows of kisses, *thirty four* in all!

On Saturday, 9 September, he wrote his last letter to his sister:

'It is very hot just now, dear. Nearly all my photos were spoilt, especially the one of Mum and Dad. It is the blue dye come out of my wallet, caused by sweating.'

Frances must have asked him if he remembered kissing her goodnight at the top of the stairs in our home in Leeds. He wrote:

'Do I remember kissing you goodnight? Of course, dear. Perhaps we will soon be together again, kissing you goodnight and wishing pleasant dreams.'

His last words to her were:

'Well, dear, must close now. Cheerio. Keep your chin up. All my love and kisses from x x x x x x Your loving brother x x and kisses to niece Anne from her Uncle Bill x x x x x x x x x x x x x x x x x x x x x x x.'

Four days later he was dead.

At the bottom of the bundle of letters I found a tiny scrap of yellow paper. It was the dreadful telegram which Will's young wife, Molly, had sent to Dad, who was serving with the Scots Guards in Caernarvon.

'RECEIVED NEWS BILL MISSING BELIEVED KILLED. PLEASE TELL FRANCES. WRITING TO HER. MOLLY.'

She obviously knew what a great shock this would be to Frances, so she left it to Dad to break the devastating news.

Reading through his letters once more, I found myself wondering what would have become of my uncle had he gone to Canada on the Child Migrant Scheme, instead of going through the hell of war to his death at Coriano Ridge in 1944. Then I had a strange thought. Had he gone to Canada, he might well have joined the Canadian Army. Many of their lads ended up in the same Italian cemetery at Gradara, where Will is buried. So perhaps his fate would have been the same. Perhaps, for 'this little chap', all roads led to Italy on 13 September, 1944. It's a curious thought.

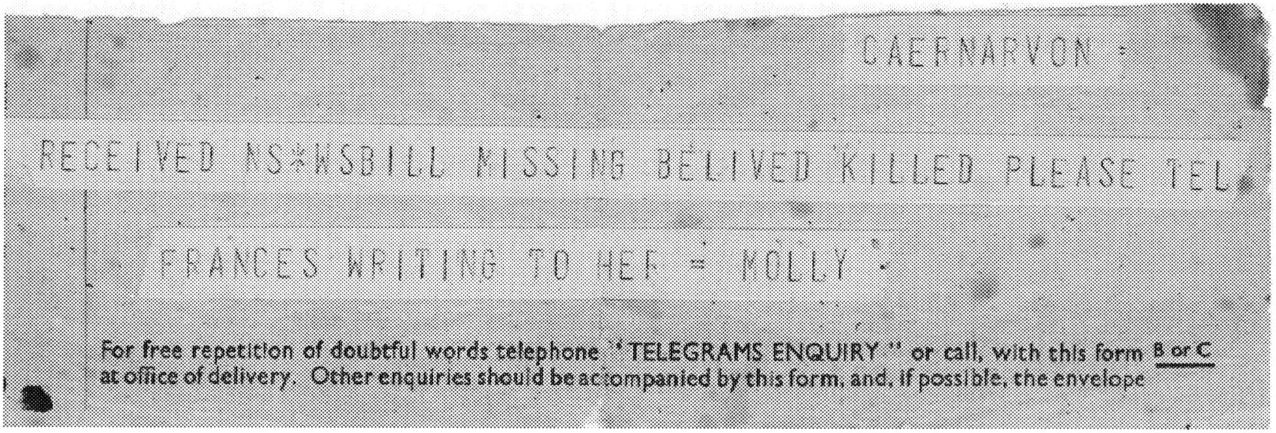

CAERNARVON =

RECEIVED NS*WSBILL MISSING BELIVED KILLED PLEASE TEL

FRANCES WRITING TO HER = MOLLY :

For free repetition of doubtful words telephone "TELEGRAMS ENQUIRY" or call, with this form B or C at office of delivery. Other enquiries should be accompanied by this form, and, if possible, the envelope

CHAPTER FIVE

ONCE A FUSILIER, ALWAYS A FUSILIER

As I still felt I knew so little about Mum's little brother, I was now consumed by a desire to find someone who knew him during his army service. A long shot, this, for over fifty years have passed and many old soldiers have gone to their well-earned rest. Nevertheless, the Miss Marple hidden inside me would not lie down and be quiet. I thought how wonderful it would be if we could have some first-hand anecdotes from his old comrades.

First I tried Major Swift at Kneller Hall, where army bandsmen are trained. I sent a copy of one of Mum's photographs, showing her brother in a group of bandsmen. Clever stuff, I thought. That idea took off like a lead balloon! Major Swift told me that the photograph showed not a regimental band but a Corps of Drums, which would be taught by a regimental Drum Major, not at Kneller Hall. Mum had already told me that Will played the bugle. Now I had discovered that he would also have been taught the drums and fife, but no records would have survived. How frustrating. Never mind – try again.

A long-serving member of my Swarthmore Family History Class, Leslie McHugh, who is a modest expert on the Battle of the Somme, was very helpful in putting me in touch with his friend, Dr. Arthur Potten, who had himself done some research on the Royal Fusiliers. It was this contact with Arthur Potten which set the wheels of my research rolling in earnest. The trail was to lead me from Arthur to Jim, and thence via Jack, Tony and Alf, to Ted, who was able to tell me, 'I was there the day your uncle died!'

But that was all in the future. Family history research progresses in bursts of activity and nail-biting inactivity. The uncovering of my uncle's story was to take about a year and a half. It all began with Arthur, who gave me the first pieces of the jigsaw. He spent many hours researching on my behalf, and was then able to tell me exactly where Will Harrap's battalion served, which medals he earned and the name of the place where he died – Coriano Ridge, not far from Rimini on the Adriatic coast. Among the list of his medals was one called the Italy Star. As that was where he died, I thought it would be good to try to obtain one for Mum, in memory of her little brother.

One evening, after giving a talk on 'My Gallant Hussar' to the Horbury Medals Society, I asked

Regimental Corps of Drums. (Will second row, third from left).

their advice about getting an Italy Star. Ted Andrassy offered to buy one for us and have it mounted and framed by one of his fellow members. Eventually I received Will's medal, beautifully framed by Joe Hammerton. Mounted with the medal was the happy photograph taken on his wedding day. It now has pride of place on the wall opposite Mum's armchair, where she can see his smiling face every day.

Many years ago, when she was younger and fitter, she had gone to Italy with my father in order to visit Gradara Cemetery where her beloved brother was buried. After a hair-raising journey, on their own and with not one word of Italian between them, they were directed by a railway signalman, '– so many kilometres' and he pointed up a long and dusty road. As Mum says, they had no idea how far a kilometre was. It could have been a hundred miles for all they knew!

These two 'innocents abroad' then set off up the road in the blazing August sun, to find Gradara. Eventually they reached their goal and, after a long search, stood before Will's stone. The inscription reads:

6457266 FUSILIER
W. S. HARRAP
THE ROYAL FUSILIERS
13th SEPTEMBER 1944 age 29
\+
'TILL THE DAY BREAK
YOU WILL BE FOR EVER
IN OUR THOUGHTS'

It must have been overwhelmingly sad for Frances, but I know it brings her some comfort, even now, to know that she had been able to say her last farewell to her little brother.

Some photographs were taken on that hot August day, but the fierce sun bleached out almost all the details on the resulting pictures. I decided that Mum should have a decent photograph of the grave, so I sent all the details I had to the War Graves Commission, who provided us with not one but three beautiful clear photographs.

I am always amazed, when researching, at the long arm of coincidence. I gave a Family History talk recently to

the Chevin Antiques Society at Bramhope, and was chatting afterwards to an elderly gentleman called Derek Fall. The conversation turned to my current research of my Fusilier. 'I was in the Royal Fusiliers,' he said. 'Not the 2nd Battalion, by any chance?' I asked. 'Yes! I was injured in the leg so badly that I was sent home from Italy in 1944.' I couldn't believe my ears when he named the battle in which he had been injured. 'It was at Coriano Ridge.' 'Not in *September*, 1944?' I asked. 'Yes,' said

Derek, 'It was the 13th.' How absolutely amazing! That was the very place and date Will Harrap was killed.

Sadly, he did not remember him personally, but I still had this profound optimism that if I tried hard enough I would find an old comrade who did remember him. After all, I did find Mabel Wood's Madonna! So I wrote to the British Legion and asked them to publish a plea for help in their magazine. 'Do you remember Will Harrap, Royal Fusiliers, killed in Italy, September 1944?'

Some weeks later Simon, my postie, brought me a letter from a lady in Devon. She wrote:

> 'How strange to see that name in the British Legion magazine. I knew him when I was a young land-girl living in the same village as Molly . . . I saw Molly and Bill marry, and was there when the "missing believed killed" letter came . . . I knew his daughter Hazel from birth. The last time I saw her she was about ten. She'd be in her fifties now?'

The writer was a lady called Mary Gosden. She went on to provide me with a lovely word-portrait of my uncle:

> 'Bill was a nice man, genuine, quiet, in fact ordinary, except for one thing. He had the most infectious laugh I'd ever heard. This is how I still remember him, as a 73-year-old now, just for that laugh that made everyone near laugh too.'

This is what I had longed for – a first-hand account of my 'little chap' as a grown man.

In a later letter Mary told me that she had been engaged to a Canadian soldier, Bill Holden, who knew Bill/Will Harrap well. Her Bill was also killed in Italy, about a month after my Fusilier. Shortly before that he had told her, in a letter, that the two soldier friends had met up again in Rome, where they were both on leave.

She shared with me her memories of Will and Molly's wedding and the little party afterwards, and:

> 'I can remembering him leaving on a King Alfred bus, waving like mad, as he and Molly went to Winchester Station . . . I liked him very much. We had one thing in common, apart from a zany sense of humour, we both had a sister called Frances.'

How lovely that he is remembered for his laughter. Bless him, he had little to laugh at in his early days. It would not have been surprising if he had grown up into a disturbed individual after such an unsettled childhood.

Instead, it is this nice, quiet, laughing man who is remembered. Interesting that his sister, too, has the same manner. As a young woman, she tells me, the postman used to call her, 'Smiler'. Even now, after a life which has contained its share of troubles and pain, she is a great giggler, and her photographs at eighty-four still show a radiant smile.

Meanwhile, Arthur Potten continued to send me helpful letters about the Fusiliers, including one which

Will and Molly on their wedding day in 1943.

mentioned the regimental museum at Her Majesty's Tower of London. I quickly wrote one of my famous grovelling letters – 'Dear Sir or Madam. I know you must be awfully busy, but -' and received by return post the first of many helpful letters from the Archivist, Jim Kelleher. He was a mine of information, answering dozens of questions from me; identifying Will Harrap's uniform badges from the photographs I sent; sending me pages from the Second Battalion's War Diaries for the fateful month of September, 1944, and an illustrated map of the travels of the Battalion between 1939-45.

He invited me to visit the museum and arranged for a pass to be waiting for me at the Gatehouse of the Tower. I walked in, past Traitors' Gate, where I shuddered as I remembered Robert Devereux, Earl of Essex, employer of my Daniel Bachiler in 1590, entering through that gate on his journey to Tower Green and the block. I just couldn't resist asking a passing Yeoman Warder where the Earl would have been imprisoned awaiting his appointment with the headsman. He led me through a 'NO ENTRY' sign and showed me the very house where he was held. Poor Robert. What a way to go!

Then I found the Royal Fusiliers Museum and spent a fascinating and moving time examining the exhibits, especially those covering their time in Italy in 1944. Jim Kelleher was not on duty that day, but the lady at the desk gave me directions to the Fusiliers' church, Holy Sepulchre near Holborn Viaduct, where eventually I was able to see my uncle's name, 'HARRAP, William S.' in the Book of Remembrance. In my mind's eye, as I stood there, I saw the sweet-faced little chap of twelve and the smiling soldier bridegroom in Mum's photograph. Here was the sad end of his story.

At Christmas I received a mysterious padded envelope from the Tower of London. Inside were two beautiful embroidered blazer-badges, one of the Fusiliers' regimental badge and the other bearing the Tudor rose, crown and royal motto, *Honi soit qui mal y pense,* on an encircling garter. I mounted them in a frame along with the smiling bridegroom photograph, and gave them place of honour on my bookcase. Along with the badges came a slim book, with the grand title, *The 2nd. Battalion Royal Fusiliers (City of London Regiment) in North Africa, Italy and Greece, March 1943 – May 1945.* Jim Kelleher had inscribed it:

'To Anne Batchelor
In memory of William Harrap
'Once a Fusilier, always a Fusilier.'

What a very kind and thoughtful gesture.

I was still frustrated by my failure to find any old comrades of my uncle, so I decided to try Teletext again. Surely someone would spot my request and remember young Will Harrap? The Teletext service provides a wonderful contact point for families who have lost touch with each other, or for old comrades who went to hell and back with each other.

I must admit, I use it a great deal in my researches. Every Monday morning, when about thirty new pages of advertisements appear, I can be found with my breakfast tray on my knee, eyes glued to the screen and a glazed expression on my face, as I speed-read the cries for help.

I do have a few smiles, too. One morning I read, 'Seeking contact with old *fiends* from the past', and 'Seeking Jim Bloggs, liked to be called Fred, otherwise known as David.' No wonder we have problems tracking people down!

I did have just one reply. It was an anonymous letter from someone who signed himself, 'An old Fusilier'. Among his souvenirs he had an R.F. Chronicle, dated Dec. 1944, which carried, in its 'Killed in Action' section, '6457266 Fus. Harrap, W. S.' He also sent me the address of the Museum at the Tower. It was all information which I already had, but how kind of this old soldier to take the trouble to write.

I contacted my friend at the Tower again, and asked Jim whether there was an Old Comrades' Association who might help me. He put me in touch with someone called Jack Stephens. I sent a photograph of Will Harrap, and asked for it to be passed around at a meeting of the Association. In a warm and friendly reply, he mentioned that the members of the regiment had made a return visit to Monte Cassino some time ago, and offered to lend me a copy of their video of the visit. How very kind of him! After all, he really had no idea whether I could be trusted with something so precious.

When the video arrived, I looked through it to find the best parts to show to my mother on Remembrance Sunday. It was a most touching experience. A small group of old soldiers, many still ramrod straight, conducted dignified services in numerous military cemeteries, paying tribute to the friends who never went home. On their pilgrimage of remembrance they took with them two young buglers from the present regiment who played the Last Post at each ceremony. I was reminded of young Will Harrap, who himself played the Last Post many times. These lads were probably about his age. He died at only twenty-nine, but I was told that '– he was one of the old ones. Many were much younger.'

The scene at Cassino Cemetery was so beautiful, with the vivid colours of the flowers on the carefully tended graves, the bright sunshine and singing birds, so different from '– this dump' – full of flies described by my uncle. The old soldiers looked a fine, smart body of men, their medals shining in the sunshine, representing hours, days and weeks of mud, death and destruction. Their dark blazers and berets were a far cry from what they wore on their last visit to Cassino – sweaty, bloodstained uniforms. During their short ceremony I found their periods of silence almost unbearable, as their faces showed the memories they were replaying in their heads.

Then came the familiar lines,

'They grow not old as we who are left grow old:
Age shall not weary them, nor the years condemn.
At the going down of the sun and in the morning
We will remember them.'

The choked voices of the old comrades and their wives echoed, 'We will remember them.'

Thinking so much about my uncle as I research his life, I find it hard to believe that, had he survived, he would now be in his eighties. Indeed, *he* grows not old, but remains the handsome young soldier who smiles from his photograph.

Seeing the monastery of Monte Cassino, high above the town, looking so spectacular in the bright sunshine, it was hard to imagine what Hell it was fifty years before.

Nearby, in the cemetery at Anzio, the camera picked out the gravestone of Fusilier Gillett with this inscription:

'May the joys he missed on earth
Be found in the kingdom of Heaven.'

Poor young lad, he was never able to experience the joy of returning home to his family, nor the contentment of a peaceful old age.

At the end of Jack Stephens' video was a sequence filmed at the last-night party at the end of the 'Return to Cassino' pilgrimage. During that party, one of the old Fusiliers, Tony Iacoppi, sang a song which brought tears to my eyes. He himself had written the words, to the tune of *Lili Marlene*. The song was based on the derogatory title given to the soldiers of the Italian campaign by Lady Astor. She called them 'The D-Day Dodgers', implying that they had gone swanning off to the sunny Mediterranean to have a good time and an easy war, to avoid having to take part in the dangerous D-Day landings.

In his gentle voice, Tony sang:

'We disembarked at Naples in 1944
We were young and willing and quite eager for this war.
Up to the mountains we were sent.
Our feet were sore, our backs were bent.
We occupied these sangers on top of Italy.

'We soon began to realise that this was not much fun.
Where's the *Dolce Vita* and the hot Italian sun?
Cold bully-beef and luke-warm tea,
Me Mum's not here to comfort me.
We were the D-Day Dodgers on top of Italy.

'Our officers, God bless them, when they realised our plight,
Took us to new billets in the middle of the night.
When we awoke to greet the sun
We realised we'd just been done,
For we were in Cassino. Cor blimey, what's that smell?

'Our neighbours were quite noisy, they kept us up all night,
We simply ignored them or there might have been a fight.
They did not like us, we could tell,
For when we waved they'd start to shell,
For we were in Cassino in southern Italy.

'We went to lots of parties at the ration dump,
All doing the conga with our Corporal in the front.
Boots wrapped in sandbags, stealthily,
Wish you were here instead of me.
I've just forgot the password – don't shoot – it's only me!

'They sent us on vacation – seven days in Rome,
But they didn't tell us the Germans were at home!
Cross the Rapido, on your way,
Cut Highway Six, enjoy your stay.
We were the D-Day Dodgers in sunny Italy.

'We've come back to remember the friends we buried here.
When they say "D-Day Dodgers" I am pleased that they can't hear.
So raise your glasses – here's a toast –
To absent friends, they gave the most.
They were the D-Day Dodgers, asleep in Italy.'

Tony showed my photograph of Will Harrap to a group of men at a reunion of old comrades at the Tower of London, and came up with someone who, like my uncle, was a signaller with the 2nd Battalion. Alf Adams' letter thrilled me to bits. He wrote:

> 'I met Bill on several occasions . . . I remember with regret the day he was killed, when Bill had the misfortune to tread on a mine. Corporal Pearson was also wounded in the chest . . . and he died . . . Years tend to dull one's memory. I am now seventy-six, but we will never forget our comrades . . . Thank *you* for not forgetting . . . *We will never forget our fallen comrades.'*

Alf sent me a copy of a newspaper cutting. It was an interview by Arthur Helliwell of two signallers at Cassino – Corp. Charles Cave and Private *Alf Adams!* It gives a graphic description of the life of a signaller. After twelve days in the ruins of Cassino, they reckoned to have done 250 communication line repairs. The article continues:

> 'Every night they were out crawling on their hands and knees among rubble and craters, often within a few yards of the Germans as they searched for faults and breaks in the signal lines. Scores of phone wires snake through the jungle of debris that was Cassino. Some of them run in bundles of a dozen or more and it is a nightmare job searching for the right spot in the right wire in inky darkness when you know that Germans will hose the area with Spandau fire at the slightest sound. Repair teams work in couples. One man carries a tommy-gun to deal with enemy patrols they may encounter prowling among the ruins, and the other has tools and a portable telephone to tap the wires and locate the break. "It's a funny sort of job," said Corporal Cave, "but we are too busy to feel scared".'

'A funny sort of job'! What a priceless piece of English understatement. It reminds me of the words of Colonel Marling of the 18th Hussars, writing in his diary about the dreadful living conditions during the Boer War, including flies so thick on the spoon that they had to be pushed off with the hand before the food could be eaten; drinking water in which Boer corpses floated, and the prospect of having to eat their sick horses when food ran out. Col. Marling wrote, 'In spite of everything, we manage to keep pretty jolly!'

At the bottom of the newspaper cutting which he had sent me, Alf Adams added, 'Regretfully Charlie Cave was killed beside me in a later action.' It must have been like losing a brother.

I was now 'cooking with gas', as the Americans say. I felt I was on a winning streak. I knew now that I *was* going to get the whole story of my uncle's last day. As Alf had mentioned that Cpl. Pearson had been with my uncle when he was killed, I wrote once more to my friends at Teletext, not requesting someone who knew *Will Harrap*, but, instead, asking if anyone remembered the death of Corporal Pearson. If they did, perhaps they might remember Will as well.

My postie brought me the result – one brief but wonderful letter. It simply said:

> 'Re. your enquiry on Service Pals regarding Cpl. Pearson. I am an ex-member of 2nd Batt. Royal Fusiliers, W Company. I was with him at the battle the day he was killed. You can contact me on Tel. No. 0151 3 . . .'

The letter was signed 'D. E. Doyle, M.M.' I was over the moon! This man must know the full story of how Will Harrap died. Impatiently I waited until after 6 p.m. for BT's cheap rate, for I guessed that ours could be a very long conversation.

Then, with a great sense of anticipation, and the feeling in my bones that this was going to be one of those significant moments in my research, I rang Mr. Doyle at his home in Ellesmere Port, South Wirral. I explained that my interest in Corporal Pearson was because he was killed by the same mine as my uncle. I explained my research of Will Harrap's early life, and my desire to find out all that I could about his time in the Fusiliers, for his only sister, my mother.

The story that Ted Doyle told me was everything that I had been hoping for – and more. The detail of that last day in my uncle's life was amazing. He explained to me that in battle conditions it was usual for the men to have just one decent meal a day. On 13 September, that fateful day for Will, they were pinned down in a gully on Coriano Ridge and suffering terrible casualties from enemy fire. An officer called Pratt came along the gully and said to Ted Doyle, 'The lads are hungry. Choose three from each section and take them to the food store to collect something for us to eat.'

Ted chose his three men from each section. One of them was Will Harrap. To reach the food store was no easy matter, for it lay beyond a heavily mined area. One narrow strip of land was clear of mines, and that safe path was marked out by a line of white tape. Following the white tape was called, 'walking the point', and was a nerve-racking, hazardous experience, very unpopular with the men.

Ted told me that at first he led the line of men, followed by Cpl. Pearson and then Will Harrap and another man. There was a lot of good-natured banter, and a bit of jocular pushing and shoving as you might get in a school dinner queue, as a result of which the order of the line was changed. Will and his mate led the line, with Cpl. Pearson following, then the rest of the group including Ted.

'When your uncle or his friend stepped on the mine,' he told me, 'they were both killed outright. Cpl. Pearson was badly injured and died later that day. I myself was flung over a hedge by the force of the explosion.' How amazing, after more than fifty years, to have found a man who was only a few yards away from Will when he died.

I was very moved by Ted's words, but so glad to know that Will had died instantly, without any suffering, and happy to hear that he had gone laughing and joking into the next world. Very fitting, I thought, for a man who was remembered by his friends and his sister as someone with a great sense of humour and an infectious laugh. Instead of ending his brief life cowering in fear and apprehension, he went out laughing with his comrades.

Ted Doyle suggested that I should speak to Major Gibson Horrocks, whom I had already seen on the Cassino video. The Major was delighted when I rang him the next night. He invited me to the Fusiliers' Remembrance Day ceremony at their cenotaph in November. I felt greatly honoured to be able to represent my 'little chap' on that special day. I told the Major that I had studied the Royal Fusiliers so closely over the past few months that I now thought of them as my regiment. His parting words made me feel very proud and privileged. He said, 'Welcome to the family of the Regiment!'

Frances had lost touch with Will's widow, Molly, over the past fifty years, and with their daughter, Hazel, who had been born six months after Will's tragic death. We had a brief correspondence with Hazel when she married a man called Fred, then the occasional Christmas card and a photograph of her marriage to her second husband. That was all many years ago. I now felt the urge to find her again and tell her the full story of the father she never knew.

The problem was – we had no idea of her new married name nor her address. The Miss Marple in me loves a challenge like this, so I told Mum that I would find Hazel for her. What confidence! It was not going to be as easy as I thought. But as I have said before, if it's easy, where's the fun?

On the wall of Mum's living-room is a small photograph of Hazel and her second husband on their wedding day. Taking the picture from its frame I found, inscribed on the back, 'Love from Hazel and Ray'. As we had no record of her married name, nor any idea of the date of this marriage, there was not much to go on. Those two pieces of information would have been such a help. I could have found their marriage in the official records of the St. Catherine's Index of Marriages. That would have led to their marriage certificate which, hopefully, would yield an address. Instead I had to do some 'sideways thinking' and find another route to Hazel.

I tried good old Teletext *Lost Touch* service yet again. 'Hazel, née Harrap, daughter of Will and Molly. Your Aunt Frances has lost your address. *Please* write to your cousin Anne at 34 . . .' There was a deafening silence. No wonderful letter from Hazel, nor from any of her friends or neighbours. I would have to try something else.

In Mum's sideboard cupboard she keeps a heap of old Christmas, birthday and anniversary cards – only those from special people. Could there possibly be an old Christmas card from Hazel which might carry a clue? I sat on the floor and patiently worked my way through the heap of cards. Amazingly, there it was – a card bearing the words, 'Love from Hazel and Ray Hiskett'. It was another small clue – another step towards finding Will's lost daughter – but where in the whole world might they be living?

I interrogated poor Mum mercilessly, trying to dig out something from her distant memory which might give me the next clue. It just never crossed my mind that I might not find Hazel. Forever the optimist! Mum kept saying that she couldn't remember anything about Hazel's whereabouts.

Then one day, out of the blue, she remarked, 'I think Molly lived in Winchester. Perhaps Hazel lives there still.' Later, when pressed further, she added, 'I keep remembering the name Kingsway. Perhaps that was the street?' What a brilliant memory for an eighty-four-year-old!

Now, I thought, this was going to be a doddle, just too easy for words. All I had to do was ring Directory Enquiries and bingo! I would be able to make contact. Merrily I rang 192 and asked for the number of R. Hiskett who, I believed, lived in Kingsway, Winchester.

'There is only one Hiskett in the Winchester area,' said the D.E. lady,' – an H. Hiskett.' 'That's the one,' I squealed with delight, 'That's Hazel. The 'phone must be in her name. Well done.' My joy was short-lived. 'Sorry,' said the D.E. lady. 'I'm afraid that she is ex-directory.' What frustration! I would not have minded so much if she had not been on the telephone, but to know that she was there, so close but inaccessible, was more than I could bear.

'Please, could you just confirm that she still lives in Kingsway, Winchester,' I begged, having quickly explained my reason for wanting to find her. The D.E. lady was sympathetic but it was really a 'jobsworth' situation. However, I must have sounded really desperate, for she told me that, although she was not allowed to give me an exact address, she could just tell me that H. Hiskett lived not in a *street* called Kingsway, but in a district called *Kingsworthy*. Bless her, she had given me the next piece of the jigsaw. Once again I felt sure I was moving closer to Hazel. I realised that she would be on the electoral register of Kingsworthy, so it should be easy to find her now. Easy my foot! It took hours of phone calls as I painstakingly tried to track her down.

First I tried to take a short cut. I rang the Leeds Electoral Registration Office and asked whether they had access to electoral registers for the whole country. Perhaps they had a clever computer which could find Hazel in a trice. Fat chance! They suggested that I try the Southampton Registration Office instead.

Southampton confirmed that they did indeed have the electoral register for Kingsworthy. 'But I'm afraid,' said an apologetic gentleman, 'we are not allowed to divulge information from them over the 'phone. It is confidential.' More frustration for me. Hazel was certainly playing hard to get, but, like a dog with a bone, I would not let go. 'Why ever not?' I said. 'Presumably, if I lived near enough, I could go into a Southampton public library and see the register for myself?' 'Indeed you could,' said my gentleman in a sad voice, 'but I'm afraid we cannot give any information over the 'phone. Sorry.'

At this point anyone in their right mind would admit defeat and accept that Hazel could not be found, but then family historians are persistent folk who thrive on rejection and frustration. That is what gives us such a 'high' when we finally achieve the impossible goal. So, still seething at the regulation which allows you to look at a record in person but forbids you receiving it over the phone, I settled down to consider my next move.

That was obvious. I would ring their local library and ask whether the librarian was allowed to search the register for me. 'Yes,' said the librarian. 'We do have the Kingsworthy register here. I'll take a look and see how many pages it covers. If it is only a few, I will search it for you.' I held on for a nail-biting minute or two. She returned to the phone and said, 'I'm awfully sorry but there are fourteen pages. As they are listed by street and not by name it would take ages to find your entry, and I really don't have the time. We are very busy and short staffed.'

Sensing my intense disappointment she added, 'Why don't you try Winchester Town Hall? They might be able to help.' Dear lady! Without that suggestion I would not have reached my goal. It was back to Directory Enquiries – 'Do you have the number of Winchester Town Hall, please?'

When I eventually reached the correct department of the Town Hall and explained my quest for Hazel Hiskett, a young clerk asked how to spell the surname. Then I heard a gentle tap! tap! tap! and she said, 'Yes, I have her on the screen now. She lives at 49 . . .' and so she gave me the address of Will Harrap's long lost daughter. My joy was unbounded! Such a long hunt but worth every frustration and dead end!

Now, at last, I could write to Hazel and tell her the full story of her young father's life. At once I settled down to write a long letter, explaining who I was and telling her initially just the story of his childhood. I did not want to overwhelm her by giving her too much to take in at once. I was careful to speak of young Will Harrap as 'my mother's brother' rather than 'your father' most of the time, for I remembered long ago hearing that her mother, Molly, had remarried. Perhaps Hazel now considered her step-father to be her real father. I was anxious not to upset her.

With my letter I sent her some photographs of Will Harrap. I thought that perhaps there might be some that she had never seen. I posted my letter and waited with bated breath for a reply. It came a few days later – on the telephone. Hazel was so excited by my letter that she couldn't wait to write a letter back. She told me all that had happened in her life since we had lost touch.

She now has two grown-up children, Simon Nicholas and Nicola Jane, so my mother has suddenly acquired a great-nephew and a great-niece. Hazel told me, too, about her childhood. Her widowed mother had remarried shortly after Hazel's birth and had nine children to her new husband. Whenever the little girl asked questions about her real father, she was told, 'We don't talk about that. That's all in the past. I'm your father now.' She told me, 'But I always felt desperate to know about my real Dad.'

Then she told me something which gave me goose-pimples and brought up the hairs on the back of my neck. Hazel said, 'Only last night I was clearing out some stuff from the loft and came upon two of my Dad's medals. This morning your letter arrived containing his photograph!' How amazing. I was obviously meant to find her.

A few days later Mum and I received beautiful Interflora flowers from her, bearing the simple message, 'Thank you for finding me. Love – Hazel.'

Over the next few weeks I inundated her with material from my research, so that she could, at last, have her father's story, and know, through his letters, something of the young man who was so well liked and loved. It must have given her great happiness and satisfaction. I was deeply touched to discover that she had been christened Hazel Frances Harrap. Molly had given her little girl the

touching. Particularly poignant was that on the headstone of Henry B. Vaile. The message of love and remembrance was from his wife '– and Baby Malcolm'. Using Teletext *Service Pals*, I managed to locate 'Baby Malcolm', now in his fifties, and sent him the photograph of his father's grave.

There was a note with my photographs from the Association, telling me that the head-gardener at Gradara had promised to put some flowers from his own garden on Will's grave for us. Mum was very touched and pleased that the grave had been visited again.

On another occasion *Service Pals* carried a message from the Italy Star Association about *their* proposed visit to the Italian War Cemeteries. I contacted their National Secretary, Graham Swain, who sent me some photographs taken at Gradara on a previous visit, showing the beautiful terraced site. He told me that they always took a piper with them, who played a lament at each grave where flowers were being placed.

name of her dead young husband's loving sister. That must have made my mother very happy.

Each Monday morning I continued to scan the pages of Teletext, in case anything significant cropped up. One morning, on *Service Pals*, I saw an item mentioning a proposed old soldiers' pilgrimage to Italy, organised by the Monte Cassino Veterans Association. I wrote them a letter saying that, sadly, I could not join them, but asking whether they might be able to put some flowers on Will Harrap's grave for us if they visited Gradara Cemetery.

As a result, in July 1996, I received some photographs taken at Gradara by one of the members, Gerry Blizzard. Besides pictures of Will's grave, he sent me some of other young Fusiliers who died at the same time. Their inscriptions, chosen by their families, were very

He offered to take some flowers to Will's grave if they included Gradara in their 1997 pilgrimage.

I suggested to Hazel that she might like to send some, too. Graham asked us to provide him with small cards to put with the posies of poppies he was going to buy on our behalf. On her card Hazel wrote:

> 'God bless, Dad.
> Although we never met, You will never be forgotten.
> Love for always –
> Hazel, Ray, Simon and Nicola.'

How fitting that she had used similar words to those I had chosen for the small memorial on Ernest and Annie Harrap's grave in Featherstone – 'Not Forgotten.'

On our card I wrote,

> 'Never forgotten, Remembered with great affection.
> From his loving sister, Frances, and niece Anne.
> God bless.'

I pasted a photograph of a smiling Will on the card, to remind people that he was a person and not just a name on a gravestone.

In Spring, 1997, my beautiful Gradara photographs arrived. They included a wonderful shot of the placing of our poppies on my uncle's grave. Graham Swain salutes smartly and, on the right of the picture, the piper plays his lament. It is a wonderful record of that moment when Will was honoured for giving his life for his country. I wondered what tune the piper had played. I was told that it was usual on these occasions to play *The Flower of the Forest.*

To fill my cup to overflowing, one of the pilgrims to the Italian cemeteries, George Perks, had made a video of the visit, and I was able to order my own copy, which included a shot of the ceremony at Will's grave. It brought a lump to my throat. I remembered 'this little chap' from Featherstone, the gently smiling teenage boy, the happy bridegroom, the soldier with the great sense of humour and infectious laugh, the loving brother kissing his sister goodnight. Now he lies with many other 'D-Day Dodgers', asleep in Italy.

By a strange coincidence I noticed that the visit to my uncle's grave took place the day after his birthday. A nice touch, I think. As for the music, I could now hear, on the video soundtrack, that the piper was not playing *The Flower of the Forest*, but *The Skye Boat Song.* This touched me deeply, for that was the first piece of music I remember being able to recognise as a small child. It had been used as incidental music to a Walter Scott serial on Children's Hour in the 1940s. I remember learning to sing the words, 'Speed, bonny boat, like a bird on the wing –' I have always loved it. How strange that the piper chose to play my song to my uncle. It made me feel, in some strange way, that I, too, had been present at that simple and yet dignified ceremony.

I eventually got my chance to personally honour my dead uncle on Remembrance Sunday, 1997, when I stood at the Fusiliers' Cenotaph in London alongside his old comrades and some of those elderly soldiers who had been such a help in uncovering his story.

There I met Tony Iacoppi, composer of my *D-Day*

Our poppies laid on Will's grave – Gradara Cemetery, Italy

Dodgers song, and his Lois, who had made the wonderful video of the pilgrimage to the Italian cemeteries. I met current members of the regimental Corps of Drums, bright-faced, smart young lads in scarlet uniforms, wearing medals denoting their dangerous service in Northern Ireland and Bosnia.

One old soldier approached me during the afternoon and said, teasingly, 'You don't know me, but I wrote a letter to you.' It was my 'Old Fusilier', the writer of the anonymous letter about the *Fusiliers' Chronicle*. 'I have a present for you,' said Stan, and he handed me his original yellowed copy of the *Fusiliers' Chronicle* dated December, 1944, containing the Roll of Honour bearing Will Harrap's name. I was so touched that he should give me something so precious which he had treasured for over fifty years.

Jack 'the Lad' Stephens and his wife, Pat, took me under their wing for the day, and later that afternoon took me to see the tragically beautiful Field of Remembrance at Westminster Abbey. It was a day I shall never forget. I wore my late father's medals, and felt that I was representing both him and my young uncle.

Strange to think that he would be in his eighties now, but to his sister, Frances, he will always be '– my little brother, our Will,' and to me he is '– this little chap.' As the Remembrance Day service says, 'They grow not old, as we who are left grow old –'. To us he is forever young and forever smiling.

'When you walk in England's lanes so green,
Remember us, and think what might have been –' 'We do remember them!'

Italy Star Association

CHAPTER SIX

WORK, A WOOING AND A WEDDING

Meanwhile, what had been happening to his sister, Frances, during Will's years in the Fusiliers? She had left St. Paul's School at the age of thirteen, having had weekly lessons in housewifery, baking and laundry at Scarcroft School. Now she had to spend two years doing domestic work in the Godfrey Walker Home, looking after the needs of the younger children.

In 1929, when she was fifteen, she spent a few months at Lady Padget's lovely home at Middlethorpe Hall, Bishopthorpe. Because of her family's involvement with the Godfrey Walker Home, Lady Padget used to take the older girls in and give them experience of domestic service in a big house.

Frances was the 'tweenie', i.e. between stairs maid, responsible for the most menial tasks such as cleaning fire-grates and making up coal fires in all the rooms of that vast house. She remembers, one day, meeting Lady Padget's father as she struggled up the staircase with a large bucket of coal. 'That's too heavy for a little girl like you,' he said, and promptly took the bucket up the stairs for her. A remarkable act in the days when most of 'the gentry' didn't even speak to their servants. He was a real gentleman and his spontaneous act of kindness has never been forgotten.

Middlethorpe Hall has now become a rather grand country house hotel, so I thought it would be interesting to take Mum back to see it. We arrived for morning coffee, to be greeted at the door by a liveried footman.

'Would Madam like to sit here, where she can see the garden?' asked the young waiter in the lounge. We sank into the depths of beautiful soft armchairs and surveyed our luxurious surroundings – chandeliers, large framed eighteenth-century portraits and tasteful furnishings. The waiter returned with our coffee. 'Does Madam take cream? Will that be all, Madam?'

Middlethorpe Hall, York.

When he had gone we giggled together like a couple of children and Mum said, in a conspiratorial whisper, 'See that fireplace? I've cleaned that out *and* carried coal for it!' In my mind's eye I saw the young, golden-haired tweenie, overawed by her surroundings, working in the fireplace. She would never have imagined that, about seventy years later, she would be sitting in that same room with her middle-aged daughter, 'playing Madam'!

After her training at Middlethorpe Hall, young Frances was sent to her first real job, as nursery-maid and under-housemaid for Captain Kettle, a retired army officer who lived at Naburn Hall. He and his wife were used to a houseful of servants in India, but now they had just three – a groom for the horses, Frances and a housemaid.

Poor little Frances, still only fifteen, had to be up at 6 a.m. and was seldom in bed before 10 p.m. The work was far too much for her, and soon she was transferred to another household. She was told later that, to replace her, they had employed *two* other girls. That made her very cross.

Her next place was with the family of the Vicar of Bishopthorpe. They had just moved from the original vicarage to a much larger house to accommodate their five children. Frances was nursemaid, which was a great responsibility for such a young girl. She was responsible for all the children's laundry, their meals, looking after their bedrooms and their general welfare. For all this she received the glorious sum of £15 *per annum*! She just couldn't cope and left after only a month, this time returning to the Godfrey Walker Home.

Being in service was rather like having a tied cottage. Lose your job and you automatically lose your home. Many girls in service had horrible lives, but dare not complain because they feared being turned out into the street. Thankfully in Frances' case she had the Home as her safety net.

I was very impressed to see, in her case-file, letters written long after she had left the Home and the care of the Waifs and Strays Society, enquiring her whereabouts and showing a continued concern for her safety and well-being. It was, I suppose, an early example of what we now call 'after-care.'

She remained at Godfrey Walker until just after her sixteenth birthday, when a situation was found for her with General Sandys, another ex-India officer. Here she served in many capacities – as tweenie, under-housemaid and cook. In fact she was a general dogsbody, preparing food when Cook was off duty, and filling in for the housemaid when she was out. In spite of the hard work, Frances was quite happy.

She particularly enjoyed cooking the unusual food. In her memories notebook she has written:

> 'As he had been stationed in India, he liked curry and kedgeree, which was rice with flaked fish, parsley and hard boiled eggs. The job I hated was rubbing spinach through a sieve – it took *ages*"

Fances, a tall girl with very pretty hair!

She remembers a walnut tree in the garden which the General had brought home from India. Her wages there were £18 per annum.

Frances then moved on to one of the happiest periods of her life in service. She went to a large house called Clifton Lawn, to look after the children of Dr. Platts, pathologist at York Hospital. Dr. and Mrs. Platts had four children, Pauline, Joan, 'Bishie' and Michael. As Pauline and Joan were away at boarding school for much of the year, Frances spent most of her time looking after Michael, their little five-year-old son, and 'Bishie', (Elizabeth), aged ten.

She remembers vividly her first day at the Platts' house. Mrs. Platts asked her to take Michael out to the nearby park, The Homestead, where there was a small menagerie containing tropical birds and some monkeys. Frances set off merrily with young Michael in the push-chair. When they arrived she bought him some nuts, so that he could feed the monkeys. He fed them properly for a while, and then the young rascal started to tease them by pulling the nuts away just as they reached for them. One monkey decided that he had had enough of this, so he grabbed Michael's finger, pulled it towards him and bit it – hard!

As the blood poured from his finger, poor Frances dashed home with him and handed him over to his mother. She then rushed upstairs, flung herself on the bed and sobbed her heart out. She felt sure that she would be dismissed at once for not taking care of their precious son and heir. Instead, the kindly Mrs. Platts reassured her that no real harm was done and that her job was safe.

Frances spent many happy years with this lovely family, during which her father, Ernest, came from Featherstone to visit her. They had dinner together in the nursery. It must have gladdened his heart to see her living so happily in a nice house with a decent family. He must have been pleased to know that the terrible, heartbreaking decision he had made all those years before, to hand her over to the Waifs and Strays Society, had been the right thing to do.

Frances had to leave her lovely Platts family when Michael was old enough to go to school and a nanny was no longer needed. She has never forgotten them, and many times in recent years she has said to me, 'I wonder what happened to little Michael and the girls?' so I made up my mind to track them down for her. Miss Marple rides again! I do *love* playing detective!

I put together a short notice for good old Teletext's *Lost Touch* page and, for good measure, sent a similar plea for help to the local York newspaper:

> 'HELP! Does anyone know what happened to Pauline, Joan, Bishie and Michael, the children of Dr. Platts of Clifton, York, in the 1930s? Their nanny, Frances, would like news of them.'

None of Dr. Platts' children saw my notice, but a young girl in York saw it and said to her mother, 'Don't you know someone called Bishie?' What a stroke of luck! What a good thing I had put her pet name and not her real name of Elizabeth. Probably no-one would have noticed that. Her mother passed on our message to Bishie, who passed it on to Pauline, and eventually my postie brought me an exciting letter. It was from Pauline, one of Dr. Platts' daughters, who still lived in York. She invited me to take Mum to meet her and Bishie, to talk over old times.

When we entered the courtyard of Pauline's lovely cottage in Marygate, we were greeted with open arms by a dear lady who proved to be Pauline. After a welcoming hug from her, she ushered us indoors where we were hugged again, this time by Bishie. Mum gave them copies of photographs of themselves as children, which she has treasured for over sixty years. Then we sat and talked and talked.

The sad news was that little Michael had died quite young. Joan no longer lived in Yorkshire, but Bishie was living in a bungalow in the grounds of the old family home in Clifton, which is now a hotel. I made a mental note of its name so that I could take Mum back there on a visit, to play Madam!

Bishie told us that she remembered the incident of Michael and the monkey, in fact she was there when it happened. 'I just thought how silly he was to put his hand in the monkey's cage. I didn't realise what a drama it was for poor Frances.'

Later she told us another of her early memories:

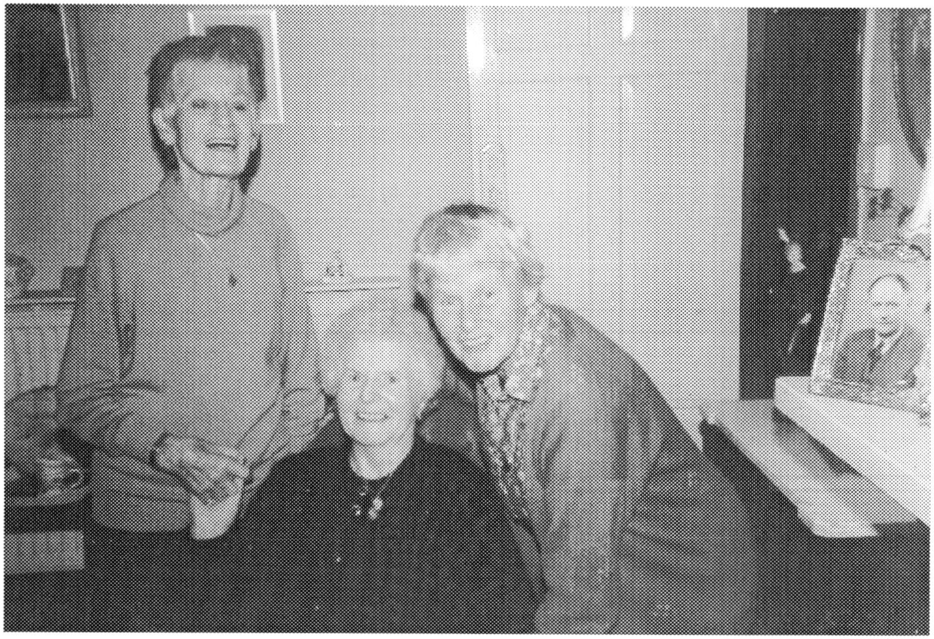

Pauline and Bishie, two daughters of Dr. Platts, meet their old nanny.

'I wonder whether you were looking after us when my mother bought me a little blue organdie hat, like a bluebell, and I *hated* it. I was made to wear it at a garden fete and in The Homestead. I can remember people saying how sweet I looked in it. I felt it was babyish – like a bonnet – so one day I put it up the chimney in the billiard room and no-one found it! No-one lit a fire there for many years, but it never came down and I guess eventually it got burnt!'

What a little villain!

Pauline said that she remembered Frances as 'a cheerful creature helping me with my horrid old school trunk'. Now Pauline lives happily with her husband, John, and in spite of painful trouble with 'Old Arthur', i.e. arthritis, she remains full of enthusiasm for life and has a lovely sense of humour. Her letters to me always tickle my funny-bone and make me chortle.

When it was time to leave, it was hugs all round. Then Bishie said something I shall never forget. With her arm around Mum's shoulder, she said, 'Thank you, my dear, for taking such good care of us so long ago!' Mum was visibly moved by this gesture of affection after more than sixty years.

Some days later I took Mum for afternoon tea at the Beechwood Hotel, Clifton, which used to be the home of the Platts family. She couldn't recognise any of the downstairs rooms and, sadly, couldn't climb the stairs to see what used to be the nursery, which she probably would still recognise. The manager, a young lady who was fascinated by Mum's story, gave us some photographs of the hotel before it was renovated. All that Mum recognised of the present building was the line of windows at the top of the house. That was the old billiard room. I wondered whether Bishie's dreadful bluebell hat was still inside the chimney!

When Frances had to leave her beloved Platts family, she went to work for the Manager of York Hospital, who lived at Haxby, just outside York. She was nanny to his little boy, John. His mother was 'stuck-up' and she told Frances that she must not talk to any of the locals from the village when out with John, for he had picked up some 'broad Yorkshire' from them, and his mother did *not* approve. Her boy's nanny had to be smartly dressed in uniform, so Frances was taken to the rather grand department store of Leak and Thorpe to be measured for one. With her beautiful golden hair she must have looked very striking in her grey skirt, white shantung blouse, black tie and black hat.

When the family decided to move to the Monk Bar area, little John was now old enough to go to school, so a nanny was no longer required and Frances was told that she would have to leave. However, John cried so much at the prospect of losing her that she was kept on as cook. This work suited her well enough, but she was soon in trouble. One day she was on her knees, black-leading the kitchen stove, when the front door bell rang. The mistress had visitors. Frances washed her hands as quickly as she could and let them in, but they complained to her mistress that they had been kept waiting and then were let in by a maid with a dirty apron! Some time later Frances discovered that her job was being advertised in the newspaper, so she decided to hand in her notice before her mistress could think up a reason to give her the sack.

The only job she could get was helping in a café in York market. She lodged in a house in Kingsway and was miserable. Her soldier brother, Will, came on leave and spent Christmas with her. The landlady left them no food at all for their Christmas dinner. Mum writes in her memories book, 'I remember I was playing *Dismal Desmond* on the piano. It was a poor Christmas for the two of us.'

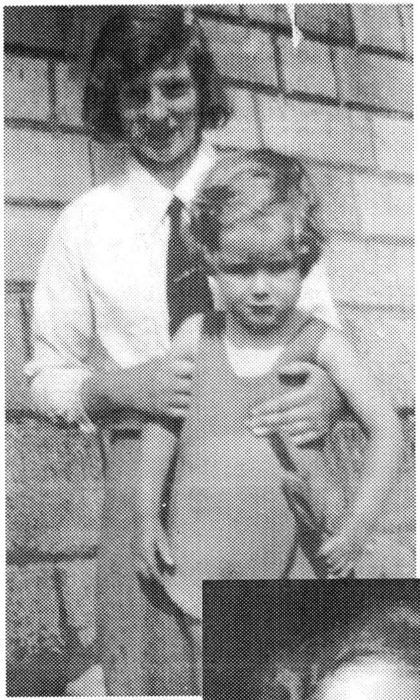

Nanny Frances with little John.

'Like a mother to Frances' – Minnie Coulson.

It was about this time that she started visiting the swimming-baths, where she made friends with a girl called Winnie Coulson. Winnie's mother, the kindly Minnie Coulson, took Frances under her wing and became a mother-figure to this young girl without a family. When the Coulsons saw how unhappy she was in her lodgings, dear Mrs. Coulson sent her son, John, to pack her cases and bring her to live with them in their tiny house in Dale Street.

When Mum told me how important this family had been to her in her early days, I decided to find her friend, Winnie Coulson, if she was still alive. It is a strange thing, but I seem to be constantly setting myself these challenges. I just get a real buzz unravelling puzzles and mysteries. It beats doing the crossword!

Once again I was successful, and was able to take Mum to visit Winnie. I always find it a strange experience when I meet someone from Mum's distant past, for the people I seek out for her are only known to me by their old photographs or through Mum's memories, and it comes

Frances in her teens with her friend Winnie Coulson.

Frances and Winnie today.

as a shock to find that the Platts 'children' are all pensioners, and 'young Winnie Coulson' is in her eighties.

Frances and Winnie spent a lovely afternoon reliving their memories of the past. It was strange to hear how these two rather frail old ladies used to regularly swim across the River Ouse with its powerful and treacherous currents. As Frances said to Winnie, 'Getting across was easy, but when you turned round and realised how far you had to swim back – by gum! – you were glad when you reached dry land again.'

Frances had eventually left the Coulsons to take up her new job, in service at a house in St. Leonard's Square, the beautiful Georgian crescent in the heart of York. The crotchety old lady who employed her was a dentist's wife who couldn't keep servants for long, so, whatever was needed, that is what Frances became. As she writes in her memories book, 'If she couldn't get a cook, I was her cook. If she had a cook but no parlour-maid, I was that until she got one. I didn't know what I was half the time!' It sounds to me like another case of – 'You can't be Frances, you'll have to be Joan!'

One day Frances went to the swimming baths and met an old friend, Ada, who had been housemaid with the Platts family when Frances was nanny there. Ada told her of a forthcoming vacancy with a lovely family called the Lythes. Frances contacted Mrs. Lythe, who came to interview her at the house in St. Leonard's Square. She offered Frances the job of housemaid, saying, 'If you can keep this old lady's house as nice as this, you will do for me!'

So began another happy period of her life. Mr. Lythe was a bank manager, and the family lived in Moorgate, just across the road from the Godfrey Walker Home. It was almost as if her life had been mapped out for her and she had come full-circle.

The Lythes had two small daughters, Peggy and Irene. Besides being housemaid, Frances acted as nanny to the girls, bathing them and looking after them. At this time she developed a talent for storytelling, which later brought me great delight as a child. She used to tell the little girls stories during their bathtime. She remembers how Peggy in particular loved the stories, and how she used to wash herself slower and slower as she became captivated by the magic of Grimm's Fairy Tales or Hans Anderson – or Frances Harrap! Frances used to threaten her, 'Get on, Peggy, or there will be no more story!'

Even after she left the Lythes to get married, Frances kept in touch with Mrs. Lythe, who came to her wedding in 1936 and personally sewed the curtains for her first home. Year by year, the two of them exchanged Christmas cards and annual letter, until Mrs. Lythe's death. As for little Peggy, who loved her stories, she married Peter White and went into local politics, recently reaching the exalted position of Lord Mayor of Leeds. Mum had followed her career, avidly collecting every newspaper article about her. When Peggy became Mayor, Mum wrote to congratulate her and, to her surprise, received an invitation to tea in the Leeds Civic Hall. That was a lovely experience, as they exchanged memories of past, happy times in such grand surroundings. As Mum said to Peggy, 'Your parents would be so proud to see you now!' I suspect that Nanny was quite chuffed, too!

By the time she was working for the Lythes, Frances had become a real beauty. She had thick golden hair and was tall and slim. When her father's sister, her Aunt Clara, met her, she remarked, 'I wish I had your looks. I'd have a right old time!'

One day, Frances met Sally Price, a girl she had known in the Godfrey Walker Home long ago. Sally told her that she was courting, but that she dare not introduce her boyfriend to her as 'I might lose him when he sees you!' Frances replied indignantly, 'I don't want your young man. I'll get my own.' When Sally asked what he would look like, Frances said, 'Why, tall, dark and handsome, of course!' And so he was. As the song says, 'Then along came Bill –'.

One day she was out walking in the town with her friend, Winnie Coulson, when they met Bill, the thirty-year-old brother of Winnie's friend, Zillah Batchelor. He was indeed tall, dark and good-looking. Winnie introduced him to Frances, and so began the romance of her life.

Very formally, Bill wrote to Mrs. Coulson, to ask her permission to ask Frances out. He said he liked the look of her , and if she was interested he would be outside Micklegate Post Office at 6 p.m. on Saturday. It was a real blind date, but Frances decided to meet him, and has never regretted that decision. She says that he was a real gentleman and knew how to treat a lady.

That was the start of a whirlwind courtship which lasted a mere six months. Bill was a York man, born in Railway Street, just off Rougier Street in the centre of York. However, he had left York in search of work and was now living in Leeds and working for Schweppes as a delivery driver. In all, he was to work for them for an amazing forty-two years.

Bill came home to York every weekend to visit his widowed mother, so theirs was a weekend courtship, meeting each Saturday at either Micklegate Post Office or the top of Moorgate, in Acomb, where Frances lived and worked with the Lythes. Being very sentimental, I decided to visit both locations.

The top of Moorgate was easy. I took Mum there the day she returned to the Godfrey Walker Home on Mother's Day, 1996. I felt that there should have been a blue plaque on the fence at the top of Moorgate, this was such a significant place in Mum's story. Instead, to my great delight, there was a modern young couple kissing and hugging on Frances and Bill's corner. Of course, in their day such things were done in dark and secluded corners away from public view, not in the middle of the afternoon with people walking by. How times have changed!

The sight brought back one of Mum's vivid memories from those long-ago days: 'We were having a kiss and cuddle in a narrow lane behind the Home. We didn't do anything naughty – not like these days! Suddenly a little child came round the corner, seeking a lost cat. She was calling, "Puss! Puss!" Suddenly she saw Bill, who said in a loud voice, "Now then!" and she ran away screaming. I was scared sick, thinking they would send for the police, so we ran in the other direction, leaving behind one of my best fur gloves which I had been given for my birthday.'

Finding Micklegate Post Office was not so easy. The present Postmistress couldn't tell me where it was in 1936. One of her customers thought it was originally across the road in what is now an estate agent's but they had no knowledge of it ever having been a Post Office.

I'm afraid that when I get a bee in my bonnet I just have to pursue it to the bitter end, so I wrote a grovelling letter to York's Head Post Office. They couldn't help, but sent my letter on to Mount Pleasant, the Post Office H.Q. in London. Even they could not help.

I eventually solved the mystery by asking help from my friends at York Local Studies Library. They were able to send me a copy of an old map showing the elusive Post Office next to the church. So at last I was able to stand on the very spot where my father and mother first met. Why was that so important to me? Because if Frances had not decided to meet Bill there that fateful Saturday night I would not exist. It's a strange thought.

Along with her brother Will's letters from Italy, Mum has kept every one of Dad's weekly letters sent during their courtship. They are very moving to me, for here I see my father as I never knew him – as a bright young man. He went away to war in 1940 before I was three, so my first memories of him are after he came home, when he was a sick man heading for his forties.

In the letters I read of his struggle to find a house for his bride-to-be.

He wrote:

> 'Houses are £350 to buy, or 9/- to 10/- a week to rent, with £25 down. Saw some to rent at 14/-, clean new ones, but that doesn't leave much to live on.'

Money was obviously tight, with a wedding and honeymoon to pay for:

> 'I am making a couple of shillings last me nowadays . . . I'm going to the bank every week from now, love, so as to try and get it all above £100 for honeymoon and wedding. I know I'll have to go some, but I'll try . . . If I have not the fare next time (to Moorgate) I know you would walk half-way. We will always manage. A friend has given me two passes for the theatre. It will be a cheap night for us both. We can be posh for nothing in the stalls!'

Another new side I see to my father is that of the romantic:

> 'I'm looking forward to Sunday. It would suit me if it was all weekends! . . . Hope your cold is a lot better. Neither of us thought about that when we were standing on the cold step at the back of the picture hall . . . I think our weekends get better, love. If only they would last . . . Can't wait for Saturday, my sweet. When we are wed, every day will be Saturday! . . . I want you to be happy, then I will feel the same . . . I will do my best to make you happy. I am in earnest, your happiness is also mine, my sweet.'

Bless him! I love the note of defiance in the letter dated 25 Feb. 1936, quite early in the courtship:

> 'Mother said to me on Sunday night that you are well liked at home. If it had been the other, it would still have been the same to me, love. You are to be mine, not theirs.'

Another letter, at the back of the bundle, was written some years later, during the war, but I found it very touching. It was signed with kisses and the words:

> 'To the best of all wives, my Frances, from her Bill. God bless you both.'

Then there is a short note added for me, his four-year-old daughter:

> 'Dear Anne, I am glad you had a good time at the party . . . In a few months' time we may get to the sea-side. Be a good girl. Bye bye, Pinoke. x x x x Pop'.

At an early age I had developed a passion for the Disney film, *Pinocchio*, so I was Pinoke to Dad all his life. The last Christmas card he sent me before he died in 1991 was sent – 'With love to Pinoke x x x x'.

When it came to their wedding in June, 1936, Mum desperately wanted her brother, Will, to give her away, but he couldn't get leave. Instead her Uncle Sam, her father's brother, agreed to give her away. Dear Grandma Coulson, as I later called her, agreed to have the modest reception in her little house.

The church they chose was St. Paul's, Holgate Road,

because it was the church Frances had visited every Sunday with Matron Mabel Wood and the other girls of the Godfrey Walker Home. She had been confirmed there and had gone to St. Paul's School, so it was the obvious choice for her wedding. Sadly, her father had died the previous year at the early age of forty-six. He would have been so pleased to see his precious girl happily married and settled in a home of her own.

Frances must have been a beautiful bride – tall, slim and golden-haired, with a complexion people remarked on. The day was not without its problems, however, for the florist forgot her flowers. She was nearly in tears as Bill's brother, Fred, dashed off to get them. Thankfully, they arrived at the last minute.

The wedding itself passed off without a hitch. Mum remembers:

> 'I was sitting in the wedding car after the ceremony. Some women came crowding round and peered in, saying, "Ooo! Isn't she beautiful!" Those were the days. I'm not so beautiful now!'

I know there are those who would disagree. At eighty-four she still has a lovely complexion and a sweet smile.

Poor Bill got a good telling-off at his wedding. First, a cousin complained that he had forgotten to send her an invitation; then Mrs. Lythe, Frances' last mistress, complained that she had lost a real treasure; and Mrs. Coulson said that he had ruined her holiday. She had been planning another enjoyable holiday at Scarborough with Frances and it had to be cancelled because of the wedding! However, Mrs. Barnes, the Sister from the Godfrey Walker Home, came to the wedding and made him feel better by congratulating him on his choice of bride. She told him, 'You've got a good one there! She knows how to cook, take care of a house *and* bring up children.' What a grand reference! And how nice to know that a representative of the Home had accepted the invitation to Frances' wedding, once again showing the on-going relationship with one of their children.

That day was the start of a married life which lasted for fifty-five years, until Bill died at the age of eighty-four. It was not all sunshine, by any means. As a consequence of the innoculations given to him during his army service in the Scots Guards, he was discharged as 'medically unfit for military service' with appalling weeping eczema all over his body, which as a child I always equated with leprosy.

He suffered dreadfully and she, of course, went through this hell with him. His illness lasted for decades, during which he managed to keep working, but it was a struggle for both of them. Yet the marriage held, based as it was on mutual love and caring. 'For better, for worse. In sickness and in health –' I find it very sad when young people today give up so easily at the first sign of problems in their marriage.

Frances had always worked hard all her life in other people's homes, so having a home of her own and a small family of her own was wonderful for her, and she worked hard to care for both. I remember, when I was little, a young man came to our house in Seacroft, doing some kind of survey. 'Tell me, Mrs. Batchelor,' he said, 'do you work, or are you just a housewife?' Mum gave him a withering look and said, 'I am a housewife – and I work a good deal harder than you do, young man!'

In her memories book she has written an exhausting list of 'Things I did when younger.' It includes:-

> 'I did all the gardening,
> I decorated all the house myself,
> Did the washing, ironing, cleaning every week,
> Permed my own hair – couldn't afford hair-dressers,
> Sewed my own skirts, dresses, underwear, suits and coats,
> Made clothes for Anne – sometimes cutting down my own clothes to make garments for her,
> Knitted jumpers, cardigans and gloves, and darned clothes,
> Crocheted table doilies, hats, scarves, even curtains, and taught myself tatting,
> Baked cakes, pies and buns every week,
> Made four tapestry pictures and painted oil-paintings, self-taught.
> Varnished living-room furniture and made coffee tables,

Always made my own Christmas cakes, puddings and birthday cakes,
Made my own jam in the summer,
During war-time, looked after 28 rabbits – to supplement rations,
Nursed Bill and Anne when they were ill,
Walked a total of six miles to collect shopping and carried it home, on foot.'

Laundry, of course, was done by hand. There was no such luxury as an automatic washer such as she has today. House cleaning was done without the aid of a vacuum cleaner. Worn clothes were not thrown away, but darned, mended or cut down to clothe her child – 'Make do and mend,' it was called. No wonder she was so indignant with that poor young man who came to her door. Just a housewife indeed! Yet in spite of the hard life, I remember her singing as she went about her work.

My father said to me many times, 'Marrying her was the best thing I ever did.' When I asked him why he never told her that, he grinned and said, 'I don't want her to get big-headed!' Their parting, when he died of a stroke in 1991, was very hard for her. We survived our bereavement by talking about him every day, looking at the many

A baby of her own!

A good marriage.

Frances and Bill with little me – 1942

photographs we have of happy days together, and laughing at our memories of the things he said and did.

One of the last things he said to us, as he lay in his bed at St. James' Hospital, was very striking. He said, 'I've had enough of hospital now. I'm going home next week.' On the first day of the next week, the Lord's Day, he died and went home to God. That morning the Salvation Army band had come to his ward to play for the patients. As I helped Mum out of my car, on our way to see him in the hospital's Chapel of Rest, I recognised what they were playing. It was *The Old Rugged Cross,* one of his favourites, which contains the words:

> 'Then He'll call me some day,
> To my home far away –'

Because he had, all his life, been proud of being a York man, we decided that he should be buried in the lovely Old York Cemetery. His stone carries the words, 'GONE HOME'. The plot, just inside the gate and under the huge copper-beech tree, has room for 'his Frances' and 'Pinoke' when our time comes.

All her life my mother has felt the lack of blood relatives very keenly. As an ex-Barnardo's boy said on television recently, 'It's when your school-friends talk about what their mother said or did last night – you feel so left out – so different.' Mum does have cousins on her father's side, but she does not see them very often, for they don't live in Leeds. I have plagued her cousin Joan with questions about Mum's Harrap family, but she has not been able to tell me any of the colourful anecdotes which are the life-blood of family history. She did tell me one lovely funny story, but it concerns Grandma Searby, who is only distantly related to Mum by marriage. However, it is such a good tale, I can't resist telling it.

Apparently Grandma Searby received a telegram which said, 'Mother died. Funeral Friday 2 p.m. – Sharlestone Church.' It was signed, 'Dot'. Grandma took this to be her niece, Doris, who was known as Dot. Several members of the family got out their black funeral coats and ordered wreaths for Friday. On Friday morning a large group of them went by bus to Doris's house at Sharleston. To their shock/horror the door was opened by Doris's mother – alive and well! They had a great deal of explaining to do!

It appears that the telegram had been wrongly delivered, and should have gone to their neighbour. Doris's visitors were left with an embarrassing problem: what to do with all the wreaths. They finally decided to put them on the War Memorial at Sharleston Church. As they were doing so, a passer-by enquired whether it was a special anniversary! I'll bet Grandma Searby and the others were spitting feathers at their expensive mistake.

I thought it was sad that we knew of no-one on Mum's Godber side of the family to provide a blood-link with her young, red-haired mother. I decided to track someone down for her. On went my 'Miss Marple' hat, and I started my search. I already knew that her mother had two brothers. One, Jack, had emigrated to Canada in the 1930s. The other brother was William, last heard of in Halifax around 1936.

Uncle Jack had written several times to his niece Frances in the 1940s, and Mum had kept some of his affectionate letters and photographs. I tried to find records of him in Canadian railway archives, but no success – so far. However, his fifty-year-old letters provided a clue to help me find the family of his brother, Mum's Uncle Willie of Halifax. In one letter he wrote:

> 'By the way, Uncle Bill lives in Halifax.
> His address – W. E. Godber, 6 Dry Clough Lane,
> Halifax.'

Bless the man, that is just the sort of clue this Miss Marple loves! A letter to Teletext's *Lost Touch* – 'Seeking the family of my mother's uncle, William E. Godber of Halifax, last seen about 1936 –' and I hit the jackpot. I received a reply from John William Godber, a son of Uncle Willie and a true, blood cousin of my mother. Many excited letters were exchanged, and we have visited one another several times.

This has brought such joy to my mother, for now she has a cousin John, who is a direct link with the mother she hardly knew. As for me, I now have an Uncle John, who rings me for a chat every week and calls me, 'Sweetheart'. Now we have met John's jolly sister, Betty, who lives in Scotland with her husband, Louis. She came to Leeds with John to meet her new cousin. The day we spent with them was a very warm and happy experience.

At last Mum is beginning to feel complete, for she now has a family, just like everybody else. Looking back over her life, she says to me many times, 'I am a lucky woman. God has been good.'

I, too, am lucky to have had her for so long, for she is the sole survivor of her family of six. Now our roles are reversed. I natter her to wrap up when the weather is cold, I look after her when she is poorly, and I make sure she has all the loving hugs she was starved of as a Home Girl.

One night, when I was tucking her in, she took a long look at the large framed picture of her parents, Ernest and Annie, with little Hilda. 'If only they could see me now, in my lovely little flat, they'd think it was a palace!'

I hope that they *can* see her, and know that she has had a good life, in spite of all her early problems. Frances has, indeed, been a lucky woman.

With her 'new' cousin, John Godber.

A lucky woman – with some of her paintings.

POSTSCRIPT

On Wednesday, 21 May, 1997, I sat in a pew in Wakefield Cathedral, enjoying a Service of Thanksgiving for the work of The Children's Society. As the service progressed, a little toddler wandered up and down the aisle beside me – a pretty, golden-haired little girl who beamed her sweet smile at all the people around her. 'That's how my little Frances must have looked,' I thought.

Into the pulpit came a grateful father of two small children, to tell us how the Society had given him support recently when his young wife died. 'Without their help,' he said, 'I could not have kept my children.'

I thought about my grandfather, so long ago, and how different life might have been for my mother if there had been that kind of help available in 1920. Nevertheless, I was overwhelmed with a great sense of gratitude for the way the Society had taken Frances and Will under its wing and cared for them. My mother is now a loving and caring woman with a strong Christian faith which has upheld her through some of the difficult times in her life. The woman that she is now is the result of the care and guidance that she had in her formative years.

When I returned home from Wakefield, I found myself thinking, 'How could I ever repay them?' A huge donation would be nice – but, in my financial situation, out of the question. Then I discovered that the Society has an Executorship Scheme which solved my problem. The Society will act as my executor and sort out my affairs when I die. As I have no brothers or sisters or children of my own, I shall leave all my money, after a few bequests, to The Children's Society. My mother has decided to do the same. It is a small gesture of gratitude for the part they played in my mother's life.

We had two visits from officers of the Society. First came David Jackaman, the Regional Legacy Officer, a charming and gentle man with a burning passion to help today's children. Then we were visited by Carolyn Mercer, a smiling lady who is appeals co-ordinator. Both were delighted to meet Mum and hear at first hand her memories of the old days. After all, she is a living link with Edward Rudolf, the Society's founder.

Meanwhile, I continue to search for some 'old girl' from Mum's Home. I send regular cries for help to Teletext – 'Was your grandma brought up in the Godfrey Walker Home, York, in the 1920s?' At Family History Fairs I can be seen sporting a badge with the same message. If there *is* one of the Home Girls still around, I shall find her! As Captain Locker said, I'm like a dog with a bone. Never let go!

Just one more thought – if you have enjoyed reading this very personal story of ours, perhaps you would like to send a donation to The Children's Society, who continue to help children in great need. To learn more about their work, or to send a donation, please write to:

The Children's Society
Edward Rudolf House
Margery Street London, WC1X 0JL

I know that would make Frances very happy!

With Carolyn Mercer of The Children's Society

Mother and daughter c1950.

ROLE REVERSAL

Once I was a daughter
With bonny golden hair,
But by the age of only four
My mother was not there.
She died at only twenty-eight.
(Influenza swept the land.)
No mother then to care for me
With hugs and loving hand.

Then I was a mother
With a daughter of my own.
I brought her up and cared for her
'Til she was fully grown.
I helped her walk and learn to read,
I dried her childish tears.
I prayed for her – and worried, too,
And shared her hopes and fears.

The years have passed – I'm older now,
My hair is white as snow,
So *she* tells *me* to wrap up warm,
And hugs me when I'm low.
She prays for *me*, and worries, too.
She sees I take my pills!
With many little kindnesses
And love, my life she fills.

Once she was the little girl I dandled on my knee.
Now with loving, gentle hands, my daughter 'mothers' me! (A.B.)

'My daughter mothers me!'

ACKNOWLEDGEMENTS

I must here express my profound gratitude to the following, without whom this story could never have been told:
– to The Children's Society who granted me permission to use material from the personal case-files of Frances and William Samuel Harrap, and photographs reproduced from early copies of their magazine, *Our Waifs and Strays*;
– to their wonderful Archivist, Ian Wakeling, and his assistant Dawn Burnett, who were so very patient with my never-ending requests for help, and whose combined skill resulted in such a wealth of Harrap material;
– to Dr. Arthur Potten, without whose expert help, so generously given, my research of Will Harrap's war service would never have got off the ground;
– to Jim Kelleher, Archivist of the Fusiliers' Museum at Her Majesty's Tower of London, for his great kindness and expert help;
– to the members of the 2nd. Battalion, Royal Fusiliers, for their warm friendship and invaluable help, especially my old Fusiliers, Alf Adams, Ted Doyle and Jack (the Lad) Stephens, for the part they each played in putting together the story of Will Harrap, and to Tony Iacoppi who kindly allowed me to reproduce the words of his song, *The D-Day Dodgers*;
– to the members of the Monte Cassino Veterans' Association and the Italy Star Association, especially Graham Swain, for arranging to take flowers to Will's grave in Italy and granting me permission to use their photographs;
– to my dear old friend Ray Carr of Staintondale for his generous help in producing this book;
– and, of course, to my wonderful mother, Frances, for sharing with me all her memories, her precious letters and her photographs, so that this story could be told.